Endorsements for the Flourish Bible Study Series

"The brilliant and beautiful mix of sound teaching, helpful charts, lists, sidebars, and appealing graphics—as well as insightful questions that get the reader into the text of Scripture—make these studies that women will want to invest time in and will look back on as time well spent."

Nancy Guthrie, Bible teacher; author, *Even Better than Eden*

"If you're looking for rich, accessible, and deeply biblical Bible studies, this series is for you! Lydia Brownback leads her readers through different books of the Bible, providing background information, maps, timelines, and questions that probe the text in order to glean understanding and application. She settles us deeply in the context of a book as she highlights God's unfolding plan of redemption and rescue. You will learn, you will delight in God's word, and you will love our good King Jesus even more."

Courtney Doctor, Coordinator of Women's Initiatives, The Gospel Coalition; author, *From Garden to Glory* and *Steadfast*

"My daughter and I love using Flourish Bible Studies for our morning devotions. Lydia Brownback's faithful probing of biblical texts; insightful questions; invitations to engage in personal applications using additional biblical texts and historical contexts; and commitment to upholding the whole counsel of God as it bears on living life as a godly woman have drawn us closer to the Lord and to his word. Brownback never sidesteps hard questions or hard providences, but neither does she appeal to discourses of victimhood or therapy, which are painfully common in the genre of women's Bible studies. I cannot recommend this series highly enough. My daughter and I look forward to working through this whole series together!"

Rosaria Butterfield, Former Professor of English, Syracuse University; author, *The Gospel Comes with a House Key*

"Lydia Brownback's Flourish Bible Study series has been a huge gift to the women's ministry in my local church. Many of our groups have gone through her studies in both the Old and New Testaments and have benefited greatly. The Flourish Bible Study series is now my go-to for a combination of rich Bible study, meaningful personal application, and practical group interaction. I recommend them whenever a partner in ministry asks me for quality women's Bible study resources. I'm so thankful Brownback continues to write them and share them with us!"

Jen Oshman, author, *Enough about Me* and *Cultural Counterfeits*; Women's Ministry Director, Redemption Parker, Colorado

"Lydia Brownback has a contagious love for the Bible. Not only is she fluent in the best of biblical scholarship in the last generation, but her writing is accessible to the simplest of readers. She has the rare ability of being clear without being reductionistic. I anticipate many women indeed will flourish through her trustworthy guidance in this series."

David Mathis, Senior Teacher and Executive Editor, desiringGod.org; Pastor, Cities Church, Saint Paul, Minnesota; author, *Habits of Grace*

"As a women's ministry leader, I am excited about the development of the Flourish Bible Study series, which will not only prayerfully equip women to increase in biblical literacy but also come alongside them to build a systematic and comprehensive framework to become lifelong students of the word of God. This series provides visually engaging studies with accessible content that will not only strengthen the believer but the church as well."

Karen Hodge, Coordinator of Women's Ministries, Presbyterian Church in America; coauthor, *Transformed*

"Lydia Brownback is an experienced Bible teacher who has dedicated her life to ministry roles that help women (and men) grow in Christ. With a wealth of biblical, historical, and theological content, her Flourish Bible Studies are ideal for groups and individuals that are serious about the in-depth study of the word of God."

Phil and Lisa Ryken, President, Wheaton College; and his wife, Lisa

"Lydia Brownback's Bible study series provides a faithful guide to book after book. You'll find rich insights into context and good questions to help you study and interpret the Bible. Page by page, the studies point you to respond to each passage and to love our great and gracious God. I will recommend the Flourish series for years to come for those looking for a wise, Christ-centered study that leads toward the goal of being transformed by the word."

Taylor Turkington, Bible teacher; Director, BibleEquipping.org

HEBREWS

Flourish Bible Study Series
By Lydia Brownback

Judges: The Path from Chaos to Kingship

Esther: The Hidden Hand of God

Job: Trusting God When Suffering Comes

The Psalms of Ascents: Journey to Joy

Ecclesiastes: Finding Meaning When Life Feels Meaningless

Jonah: God's Relentless Grace

Habakkuk: Learning to Live by Faith

Luke: Good News of Great Joy

Romans: The Glory of the Gospel

Ephesians: Growing in Christ

Philippians: Living for Christ

Colossians: Fullness of Life in Christ

Hebrews: Drawing Near to Our Great High Priest

James: Walking in Wisdom

1–2 Peter: Living Hope in a Hard World

FLOURISH
BIBLE STUDY

HEBREWS

DRAWING NEAR TO OUR GREAT HIGH PRIEST

LYDIA BROWNBACK

CROSSWAY®
WHEATON, ILLINOIS

Hebrews: Drawing Near to Our Great High Priest

Published by Crossway
1300 Crescent Street
Wheaton, Illinois 60187

Cover design: Crystal Courtney

First printing 2026

Printed in China

All emphases in Scripture quotations have been added by the author.

Trade paperback ISBN: 978-1-4335-9032-0

Crossway is a publishing ministry of Good News Publishers.

RRD 35 34 33 32 31 30 29 28 27 26
15 14 13 12 11 10 9 8 7 6 5 4 3 2

With love and gratitude
to Jesus Christ,
great high priest and eternal shepherd of the sheep

CONTENTS

THE TIMING OF HEBREWS

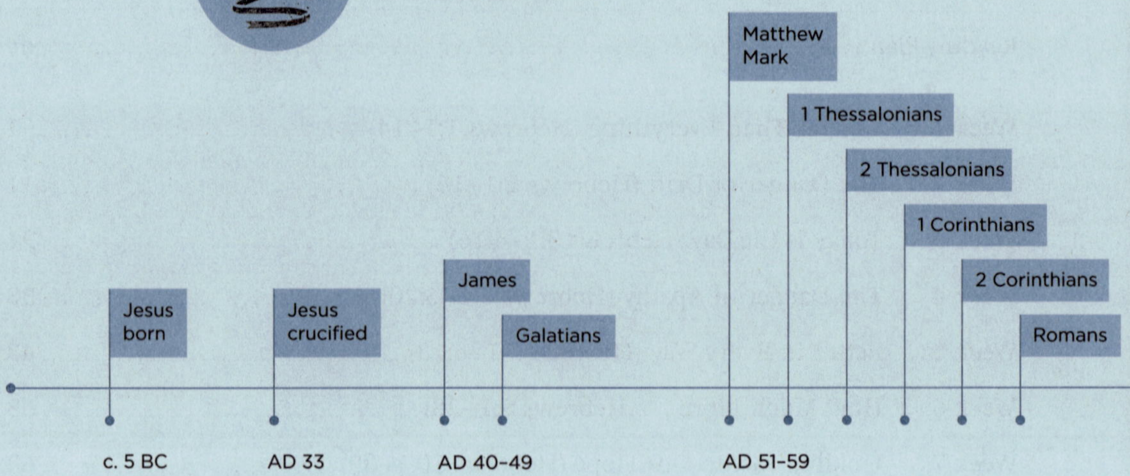

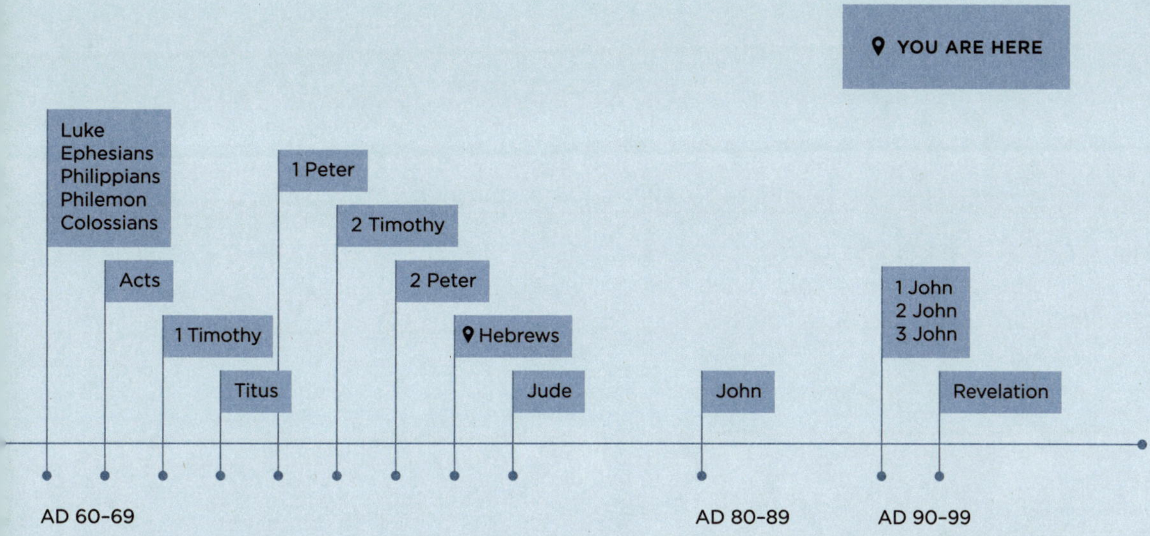
YOU ARE HERE
Luke
Ephesians
Philippians
Philemon
Colossians
Acts
1 Timothy
Titus
1 Peter
2 Timothy
2 Peter
Hebrews
Jude
John
1 John
2 John
3 John
Revelation
AD 60–69
AD 80–89
AD 90–99

INTRODUCTION

GETTING INTO HEBREWS

A broken relationship, a seemingly unanswered prayer, a frightening medical diagnosis—where is God when these things happen? He is there. In fact, as Hebrews shows us, he has promised in Christ that he will never forsake his people. But at times he seems distant, and we wonder if he cares enough to enter into our pain. When a crisis of faith comes on us, we have to make a choice. Will we stay the course, trusting him to be all he has promised in his word, or will we turn away or try to escape into some nearby yet ultimately inadequate pain relief? This is what Hebrews is all about, and it shows us why staying the course of faith is the only blessed option, for now and into eternity. We could spend a lifetime exploring the depths and riches of Hebrews yet barely scratch the surface of this spiritual treasure chest.

WHO'S WHO IN HEBREWS

The author of Hebrews is unknown to us. From the style and tone of the letter—basically a sermon written as a letter—it's likely that he served in pastoral ministry. He mentions his affiliation with Timothy in his closing greetings, so, if this Timothy was indeed the one we know as the apostle Paul's protégé, we can assume that the author of Hebrews was connected with New Testament figures well known to us. The letter was written most likely to a group of Jewish Christians. The overarching figure in Hebrews is Jesus Christ, the Son of God and the great high priest of God's people. This epistle, like no other, shows us how Christ functions as the priest of God's people and all this means for us.

SETTING

This beautifully written letter was composed sometime in the first century, likely before the destruction of the Jerusalem temple in AD 70, to Jewish believers facing persecution for their faith alongside all the other challenges of living for Christ in a world tainted by sin. The struggles were discouraging some of these believers, leading them to second-guess their faith. The author writes to both exhort and encourage these struggling saints to persevere and not give up their hope in Jesus Christ. The letter is different from other New Testament epistles. The author himself calls it a "word of exhortation" (13:22), and this is why it reads more like a sermon than a letter.

THEMES

The overarching theme is the superiority of Jesus Christ. He is greater than anyone or anything in heaven or on earth, and he is the only one through whom salvation and eternal security can be found. From this epistle we learn things about Christ not found so explicitly anywhere else in the Bible. The author shows us Jesus as God's Son, as the great shepherd, and most uniquely as the great high priest. Old Testament priests played a really important role in Old Testament worship and in facilitating the people's approach to God. Hebrews shows us not only how Jesus Christ abolished the need for those priests and their ministry but also how he has brought us near to God in a way never before possible. As our great high priest, Jesus enters our pains and weaknesses and helps us in times of need.

Another feature of Hebrews is the series of five sharp warnings about staying the course of discipleship and not giving up on the faith. Mingled with these warnings are encouragements to trust the God of all hope who will always keep his promises.

> *"Hebrews is a sermon that is rooted in real life. It addresses men and women like ourselves who discover that they can be penetrated by circumstances over which they have no control. It is a sensitive response to the emotional fragileness that characterizes each one of us."*[1]

STUDYING HEBREWS

At the beginning of each week's lesson, read the entire passage. And then read it again. If you are studying Hebrews with a group, read it once more, aloud, when you gather to discuss the lesson. *Marinating in the Scripture text is the most important part of any Bible study.*

GROUP STUDY

If you are doing this study as part of a group, you'll want to finish each week's lesson before the group meeting. You can work your way through the study questions all in one sitting or by doing a little bit each day. And don't be discouraged if you don't have sufficient time to answer every question. Just do as much as you can, knowing that the more you do, the more you'll learn. No matter how much of the study you are able to complete each week, the group will benefit simply from your presence, so don't skip the gathering if you can't finish! That being said, group time will be most rewarding for every participant if you have done the lesson in advance.

If you are leading the group, you can download the free leader's guide at crossway.org/HebrewsLeadersGuide or scan the QR code below.

INDIVIDUAL STUDY

The study is designed to run for ten weeks, but you can set your own pace if you're studying solo. And you can download the free leader's guide (crossway.org/HebrewsLeadersGuide) or scan the QR code if you'd like some guidance along the way.

Marinating in the Scripture text is the most important part of any Bible study.

Reading Plan

	Primary Text	Supplemental Reading
Week 1	Hebrews 1:1–14	Psalm 110
Week 2	Hebrews 2:1–18	Psalm 8
Week 3	Hebrews 3:1–4:16	Numbers 13:25–14:23; Psalm 95
Week 4	Hebrews 5:1–6:20	Genesis 22:1–18
Week 5	Hebrews 7:1–8:13	Genesis 14:17–20
Week 6	Hebrews 9:1–28	Exodus 24:3–8
Week 7	Hebrews 10:1–39	Jeremiah 31:33–34
Week 8	Hebrews 11:1–40	Select a passage from the Hebrews 11 "Hall of Faith" chart on pp. 79–80
Week 9	Hebrews 12:1–29	Exodus 19:12–25
Week 10	Hebrews 13:1–25	Revelation 21:9–27

WEEK 1

GREATER THAN EVERYTHING

HEBREWS 1:1–14

Anxiety takes a toll. Anyone who experiences it on a regular basis knows this firsthand. Even minor, occasional bouts of anxiety are sufficient to show us how life-draining it can be. For that reason, we can certainly sympathize with the first recipients of this powerful sermon-letter, who'd been battling fear for a lengthy time. The threat of persecution lay close at hand, like a powerful storm that rolls through in waves and intensifies after each brief lull. Over and over and over again. These struggling believers were weary of staying the course, and some of them were in danger of falling away from the faith. So, with a pastor's heart, the author of Hebrews writes persuasively to get them back on track. His aim is to strengthen their endurance and renew their hope, and he does so by directing their attention off their fears and onto Jesus Christ. He knows that the only thing that can renew a flagging faith is a fresh glimpse of the majesty of Jesus.

NO ONE GREATER (1:1–4)

Since before time began, God's work and ways have centered on his Son:

> 1 Long ago, at many times and in many ways, God spoke to our fathers by the
> prophets, 2 but in these last days he has spoken to us by his Son, whom he ap-
> pointed the heir of all things, through whom also he created the world. 3 He is
> the radiance of the glory of God and the exact imprint of his nature, and he
> upholds the universe by the word of his power. After making purification for

sins, he sat down at the right hand of the Majesty on high, [4]having become as much superior to angels as the name he has inherited is more excellent than theirs. (1:1–4)

Before Jesus came to earth as a human being, God spoke to his people by means of prophets. Through those prophets God was slowly but steadily unfolding his plan to redeem sinners through Jesus Christ the Messiah. So, with the coming of Jesus, there was no more need for the prophets' particular ministry. The one about whom they spoke had come in the flesh. Jesus himself is God's last word, the full and final revelation of his plans, his purposes, and his very own presence.

1. Using the "God Has Spoken" chart below, note from verses 1–2 how God's way of revealing himself changed from "long ago" (v. 1) to "these last days" (v. 2).

God Has Spoken

	"Long Ago" (the Past)	"These Last Days" (the Present)
How God Spoke		
Recipients of God's Message		

2. We're told in verse 3 that the Son is "the exact imprint" of God's nature. What do you think this means?

Angels

- The Bible references angels more than 250 times.
- Angels are spiritual creatures.
- Angels are capable of assuming bodily form.
- Angels are personal and moral beings.
- The wisdom and power of angels is superior to human abilities.
- Angels are a multitude, an army, and were likely all created at one time.
- The angels include at least one archangel as well as seraphim and cherubim.
- Named angels are Michael the archangel and Gabriel.
- Angels are portrayed as "caretakers of God's providence on our behalf."[2]

3. What do we learn in this passage about the Son's involvement in creation and his ongoing role in sustaining it?

The author tells us that "after making purification for sins," the Son "sat down at the right hand of the Majesty on high" (v. 3). This is a beautiful way to summarize what Jesus accomplished on the cross. Jesus died in our place, taking on himself the punishment for our sins. Before Jesus came, God's people offered animal sacrifices to atone for their sins, but Jesus's sacrifice of himself was sufficient to purify God's people of all sin for all time. After he atoned for sin on the cross, he was raised from the dead and ascended back into heaven. Being seated indicates that his saving work is finished, and his position "at the right hand of the Majesty on high" points to his kingly status. In these opening verses, the writer is setting the stage for what he's going to unfold in the chapters ahead.

4. The last verse in this section, verse 4, sets the stage for the rest of chapter 1. What does he tell us in this verse?

A GREATER SON AND KING (1:5–13)

Jesus the Son is vastly superior to angels, and now we see why in passages from the Old Testament:

> 5 For to which of the angels did God ever say,
>
> "You are my Son,
> today I have begotten you"?
>
> 6 Or again,
>
> "I will be to him a father,
> and he shall be to me a son"?
>
> And again, when he brings the firstborn into the world, he says,
>
> "Let all God's angels worship him." (vv. 5–6)

5. From these Old Testament passages, our author wants his friends to recognize Jesus's superiority. In what ways is Jesus's superiority evident in verses 5–6?

6. These Old Testament quotations come from passages that celebrate the coronation of Israel's great King David. By citing them, what is the author telling his readers about Jesus Christ?

The author continues to contrast angels and Jesus:

> 7 Of the angels he says,
>
> > "He makes his angels winds,
> > and his ministers a flame of fire."
>
> 8 But of the Son he says,
>
> > "Your throne, O God, is forever and ever,
> > the scepter of uprightness is the scepter of your kingdom.
> > 9 You have loved righteousness and hated wickedness;
> > therefore God, your God, has anointed you
> > with the oil of gladness beyond your companions." (vv. 7–9)

7. The winds and flames of fire point to the glorious splendor of angels—they are magnificent creatures! But the Son is more glorious. In verses 8–9, what is it about the Son that makes him more glorious than the angels?

The author continues to unfold the superiority of Jesus using more quotes from the Old Testament:

10 And,

> “You, Lord, laid the foundation of the earth in the beginning,
> and the heavens are the work of your hands;
> 11 they will perish, but you remain;
> they will all wear out like a garment,
> 12 like a robe you will roll them up,
> like a garment they will be changed.
> But you are the same,
> and your years will have no end.”

13 And to which of the angels has he ever said,

> “Sit at my right hand
> until I make your enemies a footstool for your feet”? (vv. 10–13)

8. In what way do verses 10–12 set Jesus apart from—and as far superior to—the angels?

9. In verse 13 we have one more Old Testament quote, this one from Psalm 110:1, which showcases the attributes of God’s anointed king. While the psalm was originally written *by* Israel’s King David, he wrote *about* the Messiah, King Jesus who was to come. The Hebrews author draws a lot from this psalm, and we will encounter it again in our study. Because of its importance in Hebrews, read all seven verses of Psalm 110, and then list the things you see in the psalm that show why Jesus is set far above angels.

GREATER THAN ALL THE ANGELS (1:14)

Although the angels come nowhere close to the glory of Jesus, they fill a very important role in God's plans and purposes:

> Are they not all ministering spirits sent out to serve for the sake of those who are to inherit salvation? (v. 14)

"The character of the messenger provides the test of the importance and finality of his message."[3]

10. From verse 14, what function has God assigned the angels, and whom do they serve?

11. How is the description of angels in verse 14 made clearer from these episodes in Acts?

Angels' Ministry	
Acts 5:17–21	
Acts 8:26–31	
Acts 12:6–11	

Angels hold a significant place in God's kingdom. These powerful beings serve God and do his bidding for the good of God's people and the praise of God's glory. Even so, Jesus the Son is superior to angels in every way.

LET'S TALK

1. Speculation about angels is woven all through popular culture. They appear as chubby cherubs on Valentine's Day cards and perch atop Christmas trees in sparkly garb. But the nature of true angels is radically different from these cultural depictions. The nature of real angels is found only in the Bible. How has this week's lesson changed your understanding of these glorious creatures?

2. Discuss what you learned this week about Jesus's role, his authority, and his relationship to the Father. Was any of this new to you?

3. We're told that Jesus, our King of kings, "loved righteousness and hated wickedness" (v. 9). As citizens of his kingdom, we are called to do the same. Discuss some practical ways to cultivate a love of righteousness and a hatred of evil in order to serve your King and Lord.

WEEK 2

THE DANGER OF DRIFT

HEBREWS 2:1–18

The pleasures held out to us by the world, the devil, and our very own flesh pull at us relentlessly. It's okay to be honest about it—living a faithful Christian life isn't easy. Scripture is honest about it too, as we see so clearly in Hebrews. The question is How are we going to respond when the going gets rough? That's what we'll consider this week as the author warns his friends to stay the course. As we'll see, these weary Christians were in danger of drifting away from the Lord, and the author is gravely concerned about the spiritual state of his friends. As one scholar puts it, "How do you reassure them when their strongest impression is *the felt absence of God*?"[4] That's a good description of the situation going on at the time of the letter, and it's how we often feel when trials linger long and we don't see tangible answers to prayer. We're going to see in this lesson not only why perseverance is vital but also why it's joyfully possible.

PAY ATTENTION! (2:1–4)

The word "therefore" at the beginning of the chapter is important because it links what the author is about to say with what he has already said. He's already told us that Jesus is greater than angels. Now he builds on this truth to show us that the message of Jesus—the gospel—is greater than the message that came through angels:

> 1 Therefore we must pay much closer attention to what we have heard, lest
> we drift away from it. 2 For since the message declared by angels proved to be

> reliable, and every transgression or disobedience received a just retribution,
> [3]how shall we escape if we neglect such a great salvation? It was declared at
> first by the Lord, and it was attested to us by those who heard, [4]while God also
> bore witness by signs and wonders and various miracles and by gifts of the
> Holy Spirit distributed according to his will. (2:1–4)

The "message declared by angels" is the Old Testament law. We discover from Deuteronomy 33:2 that when God gave Moses the law on Mount Sinai, there were "ten thousands of holy ones" present with God (you can see this affirmed in Acts 7:53 and Galatians 3:19). These "holy ones" were angels, and those who fail to heed the message they attended received "a just retribution."

1. The writer urges his readers to "pay much closer attention" to God's word concerning salvation (v. 1). These words begin the first of five warnings in Hebrews. There are certainly practical ways to pay attention, but paying attention is primarily a heart issue. Identify some everyday things that can distract our attention from Christ.

2. The sea played a vital role in ancient society. Sea navigation was crucial not only for travel but also for business purposes. No doubt hearing the words "drift away" brought to those readers' minds an untended boat unanchored and drifting from safe harbor. What do you think it means to "drift away" from the gospel, which is the point the author is making?

Warning Passages in Hebrews	
Hebrews 2:1-4	Don't neglect salvation
Hebrews 3:17-18	Don't harden your heart
Hebrews 6:4-8	Don't fall away
Hebrews 10:26-31	Don't commit apostasy
Hebrews 12:25-29	Don't refuse God's word

3. How was the gospel revealed (vv. 3–4), and what do you see in these verses that points to why the gospel message is superior to the message that came through angels in the Old Testament?

The writer's point in these first four verses is that since judgment came on those who disobeyed the law of Moses, it is much more dangerous to disobey the gospel message that came through Jesus.

LOW TO HIGH (2:5–9)

The word "for" that begins this section indicates that the author is continuing what he has already been telling us (we want to keep in mind that there were no verse numbers or section subheads in the original letter):

> [5] For it was not to angels that God subjected the world to come, of which we
> are speaking. [6] It has been testified somewhere,
>
> "What is man, that you are mindful of him,
> or the son of man, that you care for him?
> [7] You made him for a little while lower than the angels;
> you have crowned him with glory and honor,
> [8] putting everything in subjection under his feet."
>
> Now in putting everything in subjection to him, he left nothing outside his
> control. At present, we do not yet see everything in subjection to him. [9] But we
> see him who for a little while was made lower than the angels, namely Jesus,
> crowned with glory and honor because of the suffering of death, so that by the
> grace of God he might taste death for everyone. (vv. 5–9)

These verses are meant to stir up our hope by directing our attention to the time when all God's purposes will be fulfilled in "the world to come" (v. 5). Because our author is a sound preacher, he gets us there by citing Scripture—in this case, a few verses from Psalm 8.

4. Read Psalm 8, paying close attention to verses 3–6, and then answer the following questions about the psalm:

   - What amazes the psalmist in Psalm 8:3–4, and why?

   - Although human beings were created with a "lower" status than angels, what advantage does Psalm 8:5 reveal that humans have been given?

   - How does Genesis 1:26–28 help us understand verse 6 of the psalm?

Now, having considered Psalm 8, we can follow the logic of the author of Hebrews when he says that "it was not to angels that God subjected the world to come, of which we are speaking." He's telling us that human beings were given a dominion that angels did not receive and that this dominion was intended to last forever, into "the world to come." But this hasn't happened—yet. Humans have failed to obey God's mandate to subdue the earth. Instead, because of sin, they are subjected to it. But we aren't left there! Psalm 8 hints at the God-man, Jesus Christ, who would come and fulfill the mandate perfectly.

5. We can't see the full picture yet, as our author tells us in verse 8, but everything necessary has been accomplished. According to verse 9, how did Jesus fulfill God's original intentions, thereby making the promises of Psalm 8—rule and glory and honor—possible for us to share in?

FAMILY TIES (2:10–18)

The author is still showing us who Jesus is and what he did when he came to earth as a human being:

> 10 For it was fitting that he, for whom and by whom all things exist, in bringing many sons to glory, should make the founder of their salvation perfect through suffering. 11 For he who sanctifies and those who are sanctified all have one source. That is why he is not ashamed to call them brothers, 12 saying,
>
> > "I will tell of your name to my brothers;
> > in the midst of the congregation I will sing your praise."
>
> 13 And again,
>
> > "I will put my trust in him."
>
> And again,
>
> > "Behold, I and the children God has given me." (vv. 10–13)

Jesus is the "founder" (or "champion") of our salvation because he suffered and died in our place. We're told in verse 10 that his suffering "was fitting"—in other words, it had to take place. Dying on the cross was the only way to remove a holy God's wrath against sinners like us.

6. What are we told about God the Father in verse 10?

We're also told in verse 10 that it was fitting for God to *perfect* the Son through suffering, but we mustn't think this implies that Jesus struggled with sin as we do or that his humanity somehow tainted his holiness. Yes, he took on a human nature to become like us, but his nature wasn't warped by the fall like ours is. Christ's being "perfected" has to do with his being "qualified" or "made fit" for his role as Savior. The Son was *perfected*—that is, qualified or made fit to save us—by taking on our humanity and undergoing suffering on our behalf.

> *"Jesus did not come to try to make this world a better place but to make a new world, a new heaven and a new earth, and this he did by dying."*[5]

7. In verses 11–13 the author looks again to the Old Testament (Psalm 22:22 and Isaiah 8:18) to show how genuine believers are actually God's family, even though they are sinners. What do we learn in verses 11–13 about how Jesus views his people?

The author adds a bit more about why the Son had to become human in order to save us:

> [14] Since therefore the children share in flesh and blood, he himself likewise partook of the same things, that through death he might destroy the one who has the power of death, that is, the devil, [15] and deliver all those who through fear of death were subject to lifelong slavery. (vv. 14–15)

8. Jot down what you learn in verses 14 and 15 about:

   - The power of sin:

   - The power of the devil:

   - The power of Jesus's death:

We can view Hebrews 1–2 as a unit, the opening section of the entire letter. In these final verses of this opening section, the author leads us into one of the letter's primary themes—the priesthood of Christ:

> [16] For surely it is not angels that he helps, but he helps the offspring of Abraham. [17] Therefore he had to be made like his brothers in every respect, so that he might become a merciful and faithful high priest in the service of God, to make propitiation for the sins of the people. [18] For because he himself has suffered when tempted, he is able to help those who are being tempted. (vv. 16–18)

There's a good bit of Old Testament backstory underlying verses 16–18. First is God's promise to Abraham in Genesis 12:1–3, where Abraham was told that "all the families

Propitiation

"The word propitiation simply put means 'satisfaction.' It means that Christ, in His perfect life and atoning, substitutionary death, satisfied the wrath of God against our sin and against us."[6]

of the earth" would eventually be blessed through him. We see hints of this promise in verse 16. Behind the scenes as well is the priesthood tied to the old covenant, also called the law of Moses. The role of priests, especially the high priest, was a huge deal in the Old Testament. Their ministry was to offer sacrifices to God on the people's behalf.

9. How does verse 17 drive home to us why it was necessary for the Son of God to become a man?

10. In the old covenant, God accepted the blood of sacrificed animals as propitiation (payment or atonement) for sins. As you consider verses 16–18, why was the propitiation of Jesus better than animal blood?

11. Our author points out how Jesus's suffering qualified him to help his people when they are tempted. As you think about the situation of the first recipients of the letter, what sort of temptations are likely in mind here?

LET'S TALK

1. What are some things you can do or stop doing in order to "pay much closer attention" (v. 1) to Jesus? Talk about what it looks like practically to pay much closer attention.

2. Discuss where you have witnessed Christian "drift" among those who profess faith, whether those with big public platforms or people you know personally. Can you identify a pattern of thinking or doing that fueled this drift?

3. What circumstances or problems tempt you to be afraid or falter in your faith? Identify at least one temptation you're currently battling. Talk about how you will pray and what you can hope to receive in light of this chapter.

WEEK 3

TODAY IS THE DAY

HEBREWS 3:1–4:16

Scarlett O'Hara, fictional heroine of the Civil War classic *Gone with the Wind*, faced her share of losses (admittedly, most of which she brought on herself). When life knocked her down, she found resilient comfort in looking forward and declaring, "After all, tomorrow is another day!" That was just fiction, but many real-life people find hope in looking beyond today to what they can accomplish tomorrow. The flaw, of course, is that there's no guarantee that tomorrow will come. Today is the day to get things in order—especially our heart toward God—because our eternal destiny is at stake. This vital matter comes before us this week as the author of Hebrews warns us against the dangers of a hardened heart. We want to heed what he says so that we don't miss out on the reward of faith—eternal rest in God's presence. And we have all the help we need along the way through Jesus, our great high priest.

FAITHFUL OVER GOD'S HOUSE (3:1–6)

The author has been showing us Jesus, the God-man, as the firm rock of our salvation. As the God-man, he lived a sinless life, which qualified him to atone for our sins through his death on the cross. Nothing—not even heavenly beings—can do for us what Jesus has done. With his pastor's heart, the author guides struggling Christians to set their minds on Jesus:

> 1 Therefore, holy brothers, you who share in a heavenly calling, consider
> Jesus, the apostle and high priest of our confession, 2 who was faithful to him

who appointed him, just as Moses also was faithful in all God's house. [3] For
Jesus has been counted worthy of more glory than Moses—as much more
glory as the builder of a house has more honor than the house itself. [4] (For
every house is built by someone, but the builder of all things is God.) [5] Now
Moses was faithful in all God's house as a servant, to testify to the things that
were to be spoken later, [6] but Christ is faithful over God's house as a son. And
we are his house, if indeed we hold fast our confidence and our boasting in
our hope. (3:1–6)

1. The opening word, "therefore," links us back to the final few verses of chapter 2. As you look at 2:17–18, what encouragement is the author seeking to provide when he instructs his readers to "consider Jesus"?

Moses was one of the greatest figures in Israelite history. He led God's people out of slavery in Egypt and through the wilderness until they reached the promised land of Canaan. Moses is also the one who received God's law on Mount Sinai and brought it to God's people—whom the author refers to as God's "house."

2. The word "house" appears multiple times in these six verses. As you look at these verses, what place is held by each of the following in God's house?

 - Moses:

 - Jesus:

- Christian believers:

3. What caution is given to believers in 3:6?

HARDENED HEARTS (3:7–11)

We've just been exhorted to hold fast to our faith and the hope we have with Christ as the head of God's house, and following that is a warning, the second of five warnings in Hebrews:

> Therefore, as the Holy Spirit says,
>
> [7] "Today, if you hear his voice,
> [8] do not harden your hearts as in the rebellion,
> on the day of testing in the wilderness,
> [9] where your fathers put me to the test
> and saw my works for forty years.
> [10] Therefore I was provoked with that generation,
> and said, 'They always go astray in their heart;
> they have not known my ways.'
> [11] As I swore in my wrath,
> 'They shall not enter my rest.'" (3:7–11)

These verses are quoted directly from Psalm 95, which looks back on Israel's wilderness wanderings, a time when the difficulties of desert travel discouraged their hearts. Along the way, they turned against God and blamed him for their difficulties rather than trust him to keep his promises. What short memories they had! Not long before this, the Lord had miraculously delivered them from horrific slavery in Egypt.

4. Our author attributes the words of the psalm to the Holy Spirit, the Lord himself. What do these Spirit-given words reveal about God and his perspective on Israel's behavior?

5. We see the word "test" two times in this passage. In verse 8, Israel is tested in the wilderness, and in verse 9, Israel put God to the test. What do you think is meant by "test" in each case?

   - God tests Israel (v. 8):

   - Israel tests God (v. 9):

GUARD YOUR HEART! (3:12–19)

What happened to the Israelites in the wilderness serves as a warning to God's people in every age:

> 12 Take care, brothers, lest there be in any of you an evil, unbelieving heart,
> leading you to fall away from the living God. 13 But exhort one another every
> day, as long as it is called "today," that none of you may be hardened by the
> deceitfulness of sin. 14 For we have come to share in Christ, if indeed we hold
> our original confidence firm to the end. 15 As it is said,
>
> "Today, if you hear his voice,
> do not harden your hearts as in the rebellion."
>
> 16 For who were those who heard and yet rebelled? Was it not all those who left
> Egypt led by Moses? 17 And with whom was he provoked for forty years? Was it not

with those who sinned, whose bodies fell in the wilderness? 18 And to whom did
he swear that they would not enter his rest, but to those who were disobedient?
19 So we see that they were unable to enter because of unbelief. (3:12–19)

6. How does the author urge his readers to guard themselves against Israel's failure in verses 12–14?

   - v. 12:

   - v. 13:

   - v. 14:

7. The author's warning includes the danger of being "hardened by the deceitfulness of sin" (v. 13). Why do you think he describes sin as "deceitful"?

8. The author reminds his readers in verse 16 that those who rebelled were the very ones who had experienced God's miraculous deliverance from Egypt. What is this reminder meant to make them see?

9. Ultimately, Israel failed to enter God's rest, the promised land, because of unbelief (v. 19). Look back through this passage and note the attitudes and actions that the author links to unbelief.

THE PROMISE OF REST (4:1–5)

The promise of the land in Moses's day, the "rest" held out to Israel, was always meant to point forward to the greater rest to come—unbroken peace with God and unending, abundant life in Christ Jesus:

> 1 Therefore, while the promise of entering his rest still stands, let us fear lest
> any of you should seem to have failed to reach it. 2 For good news came to us
> just as to them, but the message they heard did not benefit them, because they
> were not united by faith with those who listened. 3 For we who have believed
> enter that rest, as he has said,
>
> "As I swore in my wrath,
> 'They shall not enter my rest,'"
>
> although his works were finished from the foundation of the world. 4 For he
> has somewhere spoken of the seventh day in this way: "And God rested on the
> seventh day from all his works." 5 And again in this passage he said,
>
> "They shall not enter my rest." (4:1–5)

10. What words, phrases, or ideas are repeated in verses 1–5?

We can typically land on the main point of a Bible passage by identifying repeated words, phrases, or ideas. Did you notice how many times the word "rest" appears in this passage? Five times! So our task is to understand what is meant by "rest." We get a clue from verse 4 as the author looks back to Genesis 2:2, where we're told that God rested after his work of creating the world. At that time, human beings were invited to enter God's rest—unbroken fellowship with him—but sin entered the world and destroyed it. Even so, God has provided a way back.

11. As you consider the author's words in 4:1–2, why do you think he feels compelled to issue such a strong warning to people who have already professed faith?

12. The message of good news is framed as "rest" in this passage. Why do you think this word is a good way to describe the good news of the gospel—that Jesus died on the cross to save sinners?

TODAY IS THE DAY (4:6–13)

Under Joshua's leadership, God's people eventually did occupy Canaan, the promised land; but, as we're reminded here, the rest provided for Israel in Canaan was only a foreshadowing of the eternal rest held out to God's people in the gospel. Our pastor-author drives home this lesson from Israel's history and then redirects his readers to the present:

> [6] Since therefore it remains for some to enter it, and those who formerly re-
> ceived the good news failed to enter because of disobedience, [7] again he appoints
> a certain day, "Today," saying through David so long afterward, in the words
> already quoted,
>
> "Today, if you hear his voice,
> do not harden your hearts."
>
> [8] For if Joshua had given them rest, God would not have spoken of another day
> later on. [9] So then, there remains a Sabbath rest for the people of God, [10] for
> whoever has entered God's rest has also rested from his works as God did
> from his.
>
> [11] Let us therefore strive to enter that rest, so that no one may fall by the
> same sort of disobedience. [12] For the word of God is living and active, sharper
> than any two-edged sword, piercing to the division of soul and of spirit, of
> joints and of marrow, and discerning the thoughts and intentions of the heart.
> [13] And no creature is hidden from his sight, but all are naked and exposed to
> the eyes of him to whom we must give account. (4:6–13)

13. We've learned that unbelief was the reason Israel failed to enter God's rest. How is unbelief classified here in verse 6?

14. As you think back to the circumstances that motivated the writing of this letter, as well as the circumstances of the Israelites in the wilderness, what do you think the author means when he urges his readers to "strive" to exercise their faith in verse 11?

15. What do you learn about God's word in verse 12, whether spoken, like in the days of Moses and the prophets, or written in Scripture?

OUR SYMPATHIZING SAVIOR (4:14–16)

Now we come to where the author has been taking us all this time—to Jesus himself, specifically, Jesus as our great high priest:

> [14] Since then we have a great high priest who has passed through the heavens,
> Jesus, the Son of God, let us hold fast our confession. [15] For we do not have
> a high priest who is unable to sympathize with our weaknesses, but one who
> in every respect has been tempted as we are, yet without sin. [16] Let us then with
> confidence draw near to the throne of grace, that we may receive mercy and
> find grace to help in time of need. (4:14–16)

16. We noted earlier that the Old Testament priests served as mediators between God and Israel. Jesus now fills that role in a way that none of those earlier priests could do. What do you see here that sets Jesus apart from those Old Testament priests?

Because of all he endured during his years on earth, Jesus can "sympathize" with us (4:15). This sympathy is much more than just feeling pity. In his role as our great high priest, he actually feels what we feel. "When you are treated with contempt, he experiences the humiliation that you feel. When you are bruised, he feels the pain. *He is able to feel our weaknesses with us.*"[7] Additionally, as our great high priest, Jesus opened to us direct and immediate access to God the Father—something not possible under that old-covenant priesthood.

17. How does Jesus's priesthood enable us to come to God, and what can we expect to receive when we do?

LET'S TALK

1. Our author reflects on Israel's wilderness wanderings, when they allowed their difficulties to skew their view of God. Have you experienced something similar in your own trials, when an especially long or painful circumstance warped your view of God's kindness? Discuss what underlies this temptation and what you can do in painful seasons to guard against it.

2. God's word is described as "living and active, sharper than any two-edged sword, piercing to the division of soul and of spirit, of joints and of marrow, and discerning the thoughts and intentions of the heart" (4:12). Discuss the implications of this powerful truth for your spiritual growth.

3. Are there areas of your life you've been uncomfortable to take before God in prayer? With Christ as your high priest, you can draw near to God without fear of being rejected or turned away because of your sins and failures. You don't have to get your spiritual act all cleaned up first. Identify an area of your life where you'll apply this promise.

WEEK 4

THE DANGER OF APATHY

HEBREWS 5:1–6:20

When trials endure, when we see no relief on the horizon, spiritual weariness can begin to creep in. Our joy in the Lord fades, and we find ourselves merely going through the motions of living our Christian life. Spiritual weariness threatens the health of our faith, so we don't want to linger there—and with Christ as our great high priest, we don't have to. He entered into all the travails of being human, so he sympathizes with our weariness. But he does more than sympathize—he enables us to persevere, to go forward rather than backward. That's what our author wants his friends to understand. Over time, those early believers had allowed hardship to dull their fervor for Christ, and they were at risk of falling away from the faith altogether. A sober warning about this danger is found in this week's lesson, but along with it, we're given great encouragement to persevere. And those whose faith is genuine will endure to the end because Christ holds them fast.

THE SOURCE OF SALVATION (5:1–10)

The high priests of the Old Testament, beginning with Aaron, could sympathize with sinners but only up to a point:

> 1 For every high priest chosen from among men is appointed to act on behalf
> of men in relation to God, to offer gifts and sacrifices for sins. 2 He can deal
> gently with the ignorant and wayward, since he himself is beset with weak-
> ness. 3 Because of this he is obligated to offer sacrifice for his own sins just as

he does for those of the people. 4 And no one takes this honor for himself, but
only when called by God, just as Aaron was.

5 So also Christ did not exalt himself to be made a high priest, but was ap-
pointed by him who said to him,

> "You are my Son,
> today I have begotten you";

6 as he says also in another place,

> "You are a priest forever,
> after the order of Melchizedek."

7 In the days of his flesh, Jesus offered up prayers and supplications, with
loud cries and tears, to him who was able to save him from death, and he was
heard because of his reverence. 8 Although he was a son, he learned obedience
through what he suffered. 9 And being made perfect, he became the source of
eternal salvation to all who obey him, 10 being designated by God a high priest
after the order of Melchizedek. (5:1–10)

1. Note everything you learn in verses 1–4 about Old Testament high priests.

2. For each of the Old Testament priestly traits you noted in question 1, what similarities or differences are given for Jesus's priesthood in verses 5–10?

3. Old Testament high priests could relate to sinners by virtue of their own human weakness. What makes Jesus even more able to relate to sinners?

You might have some questions after reading verses 1–10, so here's a bit of explanation. First, the author quotes both Psalm 2:7 and Psalm 110:4 as he makes his comparision between Aaron as priest and Jesus as priest (as we noted in Week 1, Psalm 110 is hugely significant in this epistle). He wants us to see that, like Aaron, Jesus was *appointed* to be a high priest by God the Father. And who was Melchizedek? He was another Old Testament priest but separate from the Aaronic line of priests appointed by God to offer sacrifices on Israel's behalf. (We're going to learn much more about Melchizedek when we get to Week 5.) We also want to know what the author means when he writes that Jesus "learned obedience through what he suffered" (v. 8). He doesn't mean that Jesus was ever *dis*obedient. His wording has to do with *experience*. Jesus is able to act as our high priest because he entered into the suffering that humans experience. And one more explanation: Describing Jesus as "being made perfect" doesn't imply that he was ever imperfect! The author is simply telling us that Jesus did everything necessary to serve as our great high priest.

MOVE PAST MILK (5:11–14)

Our pastor-author interrupts his teaching on Jesus's priesthood to issue his third warning. He begins by putting his finger directly on the danger his readers are facing:

> [11] About this we have much to say, and it is hard to explain, since you have become dull of hearing. [12] For though by this time you ought to be teachers, you need someone to teach you again the basic principles of the oracles of God. You need milk, not solid food, [13] for everyone who lives on milk is unskilled in the word of righteousness, since he is a child. [14] But solid food is for the mature, for those who have their powers of discernment trained by constant practice to distinguish good from evil. (5:11–14)

"Solid food is for the mature, for those who have their powers of discernment trained by constant practice to distinguish good from evil." Hebrews 5:14

4. What do you think it means to be "dull of hearing"?

5. The author uses "milk" and "solid food" as metaphors—word pictures—to get his point across. What is he communicating with his metaphors?

GROW UP—OR ELSE! (6:1–8)

After calling out his readers on their spiritual apathy, our author exhorts them to make some changes:

> 1 Therefore let us leave the elementary doctrine of Christ and go on to maturity, not laying again a foundation of repentance from dead works and of
> faith toward God, 2 and of instruction about washings, the laying on of hands,
> the resurrection of the dead, and eternal judgment. 3 And this we will do if
> God permits. (6:1–3)

6. In order to progress, Christ followers must move beyond the basics of the faith. What goal is in view here?

These basics of the faith are presented in three pairs: (1) "faith" and "repentance," which are about trusting in Christ's saving work on the cross for salvation; (2) "washings" and "laying on of hands," which indicate specific rites those first-century believers practiced when they entered into church fellowship; and (3) "resurrection" and "eternal judgment," terms that indicate the hope of eternal life in heaven.[8] These are salvation basics, the foundation for ongoing spiritual growth.

Having set out this foundation, our pastor-author issues another warning, one of the most sober warnings in the whole Bible:

> 4 For it is impossible, in the case of those who have once been enlightened, who have tasted the heavenly gift, and have shared in the Holy Spirit, 5 and have tasted the goodness of the word of God and the powers of the age to come,
> 6 and then have fallen away, to restore them again to repentance, since they are crucifying once again the Son of God to their own harm and holding him up to contempt. 7 For land that has drunk the rain that often falls on it, and produces a crop useful to those for whose sake it is cultivated, receives a blessing from God. 8 But if it bears thorns and thistles, it is worthless and near to being cursed, and its end is to be burned. (6:4–8)

"Those who have once been enlightened" and "tasted" the good gifts of God have been active church participants. Just as in churches today, in those days there were genuine believers alongside those who just appeared genuine but actually weren't. Only the Lord knows who's who in this regard. But this passage in Hebrews shows us how that distinction is made clear—they fall away. This falling away is more than sliding temporarily into some sin or wrestling with the occasional doubt. It's a deliberate, willful rejection of the truth, which theologians call "apostasy."

7. What happens to such apostates, and what reason is given for this consequence?

8. Explain what the author is saying through the farming imagery he uses in verses 7–8.

BETTER THINGS (6:9–12)

After his dire warning, he is quick to encourage his readers, as all good pastors do:

> 9 Though we speak in this way, yet in your case, beloved, we feel sure of better things—things that belong to salvation. 10 For God is not unjust so as to overlook your work and the love that you have shown for his name in serving the saints, as you still do. 11 And we desire each one of you to show the same earnestness to have the full assurance of hope until the end, 12 so that you may not be sluggish, but imitators of those who through faith and patience inherit the promises. (6:9–12)

9. Why is the author confident that such encouragement is warranted here?

10. What encouragement does he offer in verse 11 to those who might be wavering, and what reason does he give for this in verse 12?

PROMISES ASSURED (6:13–20)

Our pastor-author reinforces his encouragement with an illustration from the Old Testament:

> 13 For when God made a promise to Abraham, since he had no one greater by
> whom to swear, he swore by himself, 14 saying, "Surely I will bless you and mul-
> tiply you." 15 And thus Abraham, having patiently waited, obtained the promise.
> 16 For people swear by something greater than themselves, and in all their disputes
> an oath is final for confirmation. 17 So when God desired to show more convinc-
> ingly to the heirs of the promise the unchangeable character of his purpose,
> he guaranteed it with an oath, 18 so that by two unchangeable things, in which
> it is impossible for God to lie, we who have fled for refuge might have strong
> encouragement to hold fast to the hope set before us. 19 We have this as a sure and
> steadfast anchor of the soul, a hope that enters into the inner place behind the
> curtain, 20 where Jesus has gone as a forerunner on our behalf, having become
> a high priest forever after the order of Melchizedek. (6:13–20)

The Lord made a lot of promises to Abraham that were intended to flow from him to all God's people. The one specifically in mind here comes from Genesis 22:16–17, which was given after Abraham demonstrated his faith by his willingness to offer his son Isaac as a sacrifice. It's a powerful story!

11. Read Genesis 22:1–18. How does this story shed light on why the author of Hebrews uses Abraham to illustrate the nature of mature, persevering faith?

12. Our author wraps up this interlude—this exhortation to persevere in faith—with a final encouragement. How do you see this in 6:18–20?

LET'S TALK

1. We were challenged this week not to stay baby Christians but to grow up in our faith. How might this exhortation apply to you, and what steps will you take to grow?

2. We must take seriously the author's strong warning to shake off spiritual sluggishness. Talk about how this sluggishness, or dullness, gets a foothold in our hearts. How would you describe the condition of your own heart in this regard? If you recognize that spiritual apathy has set in, how will you deal with it? Name some concrete steps.

3. The author encourages his readers to recall a time when their faith was vibrant and flourishing. Talk about why such recall can be beneficial in the present. Can you recall a time when your faith seemed more vibrant than it does today?

WEEK 5

BETTER IN EVERY WAY

HEBREWS 7:1–8:13

If you follow a Bible reading plan that covers the entirety of God's word, you can't help but notice that there's a lot about priests, especially in those early books of the Old Testament. These priests, most notably the high priest, served a vital role among God's people until Christ came and made that role no longer necessary. The mysterious figure Melchizedek, whom we've only glimpsed up to this point, was another kind of priest who appears briefly in the Old Testament. We will learn more about him this week. The service offered by those Old Testament priests is all in the past, but those services show us a lot about Christ himself. In fact, everything the priests did was purposefully designed by God for this very purpose. The author of Hebrews, more than any other New Testament writer, shows us how and why Jesus Christ is himself our great high priest and what that means for believers. This week we're going to see why so many of those old-covenant features—not only the priests but also the law, the tabernacle, and (later) the temple—were shadows of a better covenant to come.

MYSTERIOUS MELCHIZEDEK (7:1–10)

Twice already, Jesus Christ has been described as a priest "after the order of Melchizedek" (5:6; 6:20). Now we learn who Melchizedek was and why our author connects him with Christ:

> 1 For this Melchizedek, king of Salem, priest of the Most High God, met Abra-
> ham returning from the slaughter of the kings and blessed him, 2 and to him

> Abraham apportioned a tenth part of everything. He is first, by translation of his name, king of righteousness, and then he is also king of Salem, that is, king of peace. [3] He is without father or mother or genealogy, having neither beginning of days nor end of life, but resembling the Son of God he continues a priest forever. (7:1–3)

1. These opening verses of chapter 7 are a brief recap of Genesis 14:17–20, where Abraham returns from battle and encounters this figure Melchizedek. Note what you learn about him from both Genesis 14:17–20 and Hebrews 7:1–3.

Theologians have speculated for centuries about Melchizedek's being "without father or mother or genealogy, having neither beginning of days nor end of life" (v. 3). The best understanding is that he was an ordinary man whose personal details—birth, parents, and manner of death—were simply unknown to God's people. So "he continues forever" in the sense that Israel never knew what happened to him. "God made Melchizedek resemble Jesus. . . . He did it by what he said, and did not say."[9]

The author of Hebrews finishes unfolding the episode from Genesis:

> [4] See how great this man was to whom Abraham the patriarch gave a tenth
> of the spoils! [5] And those descendants of Levi who receive the priestly office
> have a commandment in the law to take tithes from the people, that is, from
> their brothers, though these also are descended from Abraham. [6] But this man
> who does not have his descent from them received tithes from Abraham and
> blessed him who had the promises. [7] It is beyond dispute that the inferior is
> blessed by the superior. [8] In the one case tithes are received by mortal men, but
> in the other case, by one of whom it is testified that he lives. [9] One might even
> say that Levi himself, who receives tithes, paid tithes through Abraham, [10] for
> he was still in the loins of his ancestor when Melchizedek met him. (7:4–10)

2. The Jews viewed Abraham as one of the greatest figures in their history, the premiere patriarch! And Abraham's very own descendants, beginning with his great-grandson Levi, were given the special honor of serving as priests for God's people. In light of Abraham's greatness, what is surprising about verses 4–10?

3. Summarize your impressions of Melchizedek from Hebrews 7:1–10.

A BETTER PRIEST (7:11–21)

God's law regulated the appointment of priests, and the priests in turn mediated God's law to Israel. In other words, the law and the priesthood were bound together. Priests were appointed from the tribe of Levi, and the high priests from the line of Levi's son Aaron:

> [11] Now if perfection had been attainable through the Levitical priesthood (for
> under it the people received the law), what further need would there have
> been for another priest to arise after the order of Melchizedek, rather than one
> named after the order of Aaron? [12] For when there is a change in the priesthood,
> there is necessarily a change in the law as well. [13] For the one of whom these
> things are spoken belonged to another tribe, from which no one has ever served
> at the altar. [14] For it is evident that our Lord was descended from Judah, and in
> connection with that tribe Moses said nothing about priests.
>
> [15] This becomes even more evident when another priest arises in the like-
> ness of Melchizedek, [16] who has become a priest, not on the basis of a legal

requirement concerning bodily descent, but by the power of an indestructible life. (7:11–16)

4. What do these verses tell us about the old-covenant system—both the law and the priesthood?

5. Jesus is "the one of whom these things are spoken" (v. 13). What makes his priesthood different from what was required of priests?

6. What qualified Jesus to be our great high priest?

Apart from Abraham's encounter with Melchizedek in Genesis, the only other mention of this mysterious figure is Psalm 110:4, which our author cites to reinforce the case he is making. As we noted earlier, this psalm plays a vital role in Hebrews. It's a "royal psalm"—that is, one that focuses on David's kingship—but it points clearly beyond David to Jesus, the ultimate king and priest:

17 For it is witnessed of him,

> "You are a priest forever,
> after the order of Melchizedek."

18 For on the one hand, a former commandment is set aside because of its weak-
ness and uselessness 19 (for the law made nothing perfect); but on the other
hand, a better hope is introduced, through which we draw near to God.
20 And it was not without an oath. For those who formerly became priests
were made such without an oath, 21 but this one was made a priest with an oath
by the one who said to him:

> "The Lord has sworn
> and will not change his mind,
> 'You are a priest forever.'" (7:17–21)

"The major problem in the world and in our lives is not *our troubled marriages or our wayward children or our financial pressures or our failing health or our cultural degeneration. The main problem in the world—everybody's problem—is how to be reconciled to God so that we escape his terrifying wrath at the judgment. . . . And the Biblical answer is priesthood. And specifically the superior priesthood of Christ."*[10]

---

7. What "better hope" (v. 19) did Jesus's sacrifice on the cross provide that the law never could?

A BETTER COVENANT (7:22–28)

As our great high priest, Jesus provides a better covenant with better benefits than were possible under the old one:

> 22 This makes Jesus the guarantor of a better covenant.
> 23 The former priests were many in number, because they were prevented
> by death from continuing in office, 24 but he holds his priesthood permanently,
> because he continues forever. 25 Consequently, he is able to save to the uttermost those who draw near to God through him, since he always lives to make intercession for them.
> 26 For it was indeed fitting that we should have such a high priest, holy,
> innocent, unstained, separated from sinners, and exalted above the heavens.
> 27 He has no need, like those high priests, to offer sacrifices daily, first for his
> own sins and then for those of the people, since he did this once for all when
> he offered up himself. 28 For the law appoints men in their weakness as high
> priests, but the word of the oath, which came later than the law, appoints a Son who has been made perfect forever. (7:22–28)

8. In the chart that follows, note all the differences between the old-covenant Levitical priests and our great high priest Jesus:

	Levitical Priests	Jesus Christ
vv. 23–24		
vv. 25–26		
vv. 27–28		

9. In your own words, summarize from verse 25 the three great blessings we receive through Christ our great high priest:

   1. ……………………………………………………………………………………

   2. ……………………………………………………………………………………

   3. ……………………………………………………………………………………

A BETTER SANCTUARY (8:1–6)

The old-covenant priests carried out their ministry first in the tabernacle, or "tent," and years later in the temple. (We will learn more about this next week.) Every detail of their priestly work, such as offering gifts and sacrifices on behalf of God's people, was spelled out in the law. Even the design of this tent and its furnishings was divinely regulated, from the craftsmanship of the furniture to the ornate beauty of its embellishments. But Christ our great high priest carries out his ministry from heaven and administers a new, better covenant:

> 1 Now the point in what we are saying is this: we have such a high priest, one
> who is seated at the right hand of the throne of the Majesty in heaven, 2 a min-
> ister in the holy places, in the true tent that the Lord set up, not man. 3 For
> every high priest is appointed to offer gifts and sacrifices; thus it is necessary
> for this priest also to have something to offer. 4 Now if he were on earth, he
> would not be a priest at all, since there are priests who offer gifts according
> to the law. 5 They serve a copy and shadow of the heavenly things. For when
> Moses was about to erect the tent, he was instructed by God, saying, "See that
> you make everything according to the pattern that was shown you on the
> mountain." 6 But as it is, Christ has obtained a ministry that is as much more
> excellent than the old as the covenant he mediates is better, since it is enacted
> on better promises. (8:1–6)

10. In these verses, how does Christ differ from the old-covenant priests:

   - Where he serves:

   ……………………………………………………………………………………

   ……………………………………………………………………………………

- How he serves:

11. Old-covenant priests were required to offer sacrifices on behalf of God's people. How did Jesus Christ fit this priestly qualification?

A BETTER COVENANT (8:7–13)

Quoting from the prophet Jeremiah, our author now holds out to us those "better promises" (8:6) of the new covenant:

> [7] For if that first covenant had been faultless, there would have been no occasion to look for a second.
>
> [8] For he finds fault with them when he says:
>
> "Behold, the days are coming, declares the Lord,
> when I will establish a new covenant with the house of Israel
> and with the house of Judah,
> [9] not like the covenant that I made with their fathers
> on the day when I took them by the hand to bring them out of the land of Egypt.
> For they did not continue in my covenant,
> and so I showed no concern for them, declares the Lord.
> [10] For this is the covenant that I will make with the house of Israel
> after those days, declares the Lord:
> I will put my laws into their minds,
> and write them on their hearts,
> and I will be their God,
> and they shall be my people.

> 11 And they shall not teach, each one his neighbor
> and each one his brother, saying, 'Know the Lord,'
> for they shall all know me,
> from the least of them to the greatest.
> 12 For I will be merciful toward their iniquities,
> and I will remember their sins no more."

13 In speaking of a new covenant, he makes the first one obsolete. And what is becoming obsolete and growing old is ready to vanish away. (8:7–13)

12. How does the new covenant differ from the old covenant in how God relates to his people?

LET'S TALK

1. The Bible's emphasis on priesthood—both in the Old Testament and here in Hebrews—exposes a stark reality: "If, to be saved forever, we need Christ to intercede for us forever with God, then what is the implication about what we need saving from? The implication is that we need to be saved from God. Specifically we need to be saved from the wrath of God."[11] Discuss how focusing on Christ as your great high priest has changed your understanding of both your sinfulness and God's holiness.

2. We're told that our great high priest Jesus Christ "is able to save to the uttermost those who draw near to God through him, since he always lives to make intercession for them" (7:25). Talk about how this amazing truth enables us to stop hiding from God when we feel guilty and to be honest with him about our sin struggles.

3. As you reflect on all you learned this week, from the priesthood of Christ to the promises of the new covenant, identify one or two things that most encourage you to face a particular hardship or uncertainty in your life.

WEEK 6

HOW MUCH MORE . . .

HEBREWS 9:1–28

The weight of guilt—you know the heavy feeling. A troubled conscience zaps your energy, your interests, and all your joy. Sometimes we excuse our sin or blame-shift, but the guilt is still there. Or we try to cover our guilty feelings with good deeds, but those don't help either. Those tactics don't work because the guilt is real. We *are* guilty, and we can do nothing to make ourselves clean. That's why Hebrews 9 is a spiritual lift for guilt-heavy hearts. There is a remedy, just one—the blood of Christ, which he sacrificed on the cross for those buried under that weight of guilt. We learn more about the purifying work of Christ this week, especially when our author holds it up alongside the most important day on Israel's annual worship calendar, the Day of Atonement. We're also going to look inside the Old Testament tabernacle to see what its structure and furnishings symbolized about God's eternal plan for his people. There's a lot to take in from these twenty-eight verses, so be sure to read through the Bible passages slowly and carefully.

REFLECTIONS OF A HOLY GOD (9:1–10)

Under the old covenant God made with his people through Moses, worship was tightly regulated:

> [1]Now even the first covenant had regulations for worship and an earthly place
> of holiness. [2]For a tent was prepared, the first section, in which were the lamp-
> stand and the table and the bread of the Presence. It is called the Holy Place.

3 Behind the second curtain was a second section called the Most Holy Place,
4 having the golden altar of incense and the ark of the covenant covered on all
sides with gold, in which was a golden urn holding the manna, and Aaron's
staff that budded, and the tablets of the covenant. 5 Above it were the cherubim
of glory overshadowing the mercy seat. Of these things we cannot now speak
in detail. (vv. 1–5)

1. Described in verses 1–5 is the tent, or tabernacle, and its furnishings. The tabernacle symbolized God's presence with his people. In the tabernacle diagram below, indicate where each item belongs. (The golden altar of incense was actually in the first section, the Holy Place, just outside the curtain that divided sections 1 and 2. Our author didn't make a mistake! His wording here is just a bit tricky.)

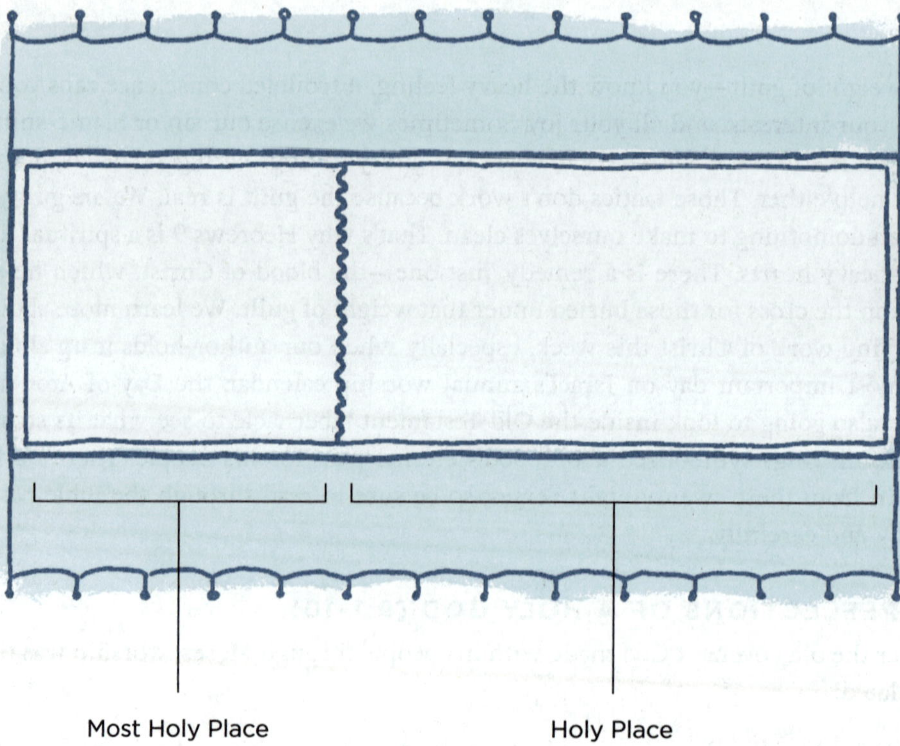

Having set the stage, we now see how God was worshiped in the tabernacle:

> [6] These preparations having thus been made, the priests go regularly into the first section, performing their ritual duties, [7] but into the second only the high priest goes, and he but once a year, and not without taking blood, which he offers for himself and for the unintentional sins of the people. [8] By this the Holy Spirit indicates that the way into the holy places is not yet opened as long as the first section is still standing [9] (which is symbolic for the present age). According to this arrangement, gifts and sacrifices are offered that cannot perfect the conscience of the worshiper, [10] but deal only with food and drink and various washings, regulations for the body imposed until the time of reformation. (vv. 6–10)

2. How did the duties of the regular priests differ from those of the high priest?

3. We see in verses 6–10 that the setup of the tabernacle and the duties of the priests were designed to reveal the reality of life for sinners who break God's covenant. What deep human need was exposed through these rituals?

HOW MUCH MORE . . . (9:11–14)

The entire structure of old-covenant worship, from the tabernacle setup to the priests who ministered there, was purposefully insufficient in order to show that a better system was needed:

[11] But when Christ appeared as a high priest of the good things that have come,
then through the greater and more perfect tent (not made with hands, that is,
not of this creation) [12] he entered once for all into the holy places, not by means
of the blood of goats and calves but by means of his own blood, thus securing
an eternal redemption. [13] For if the blood of goats and bulls, and the sprinkling
of defiled persons with the ashes of a heifer, sanctify for the purification of
the flesh, [14] how much more will the blood of Christ, who through the eternal
Spirit offered himself without blemish to God, purify our conscience from dead
works to serve the living God. (vv. 11–14)

4. In verses 11–14 we see why Jesus Christ is rightly designated the great high priest.

   - How did Christ's sacrifice differ from the sacrifices offered by the old-covenant priests?

   - What did Christ's sacrifice accomplish for God's people?

5. How was each person of the Trinity—Father, Son, and Holy Spirit—involved in Christ's sacrifice for sinners?

   - Father:

- Son:

- Holy Spirit:

The Tabernacle Tent[12]

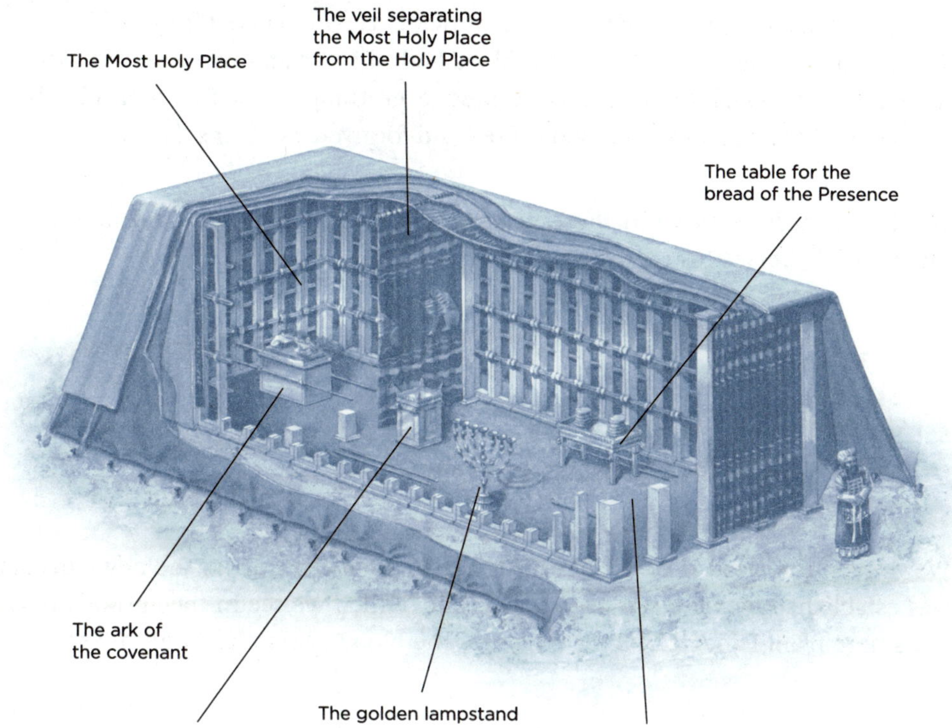

BLOOD THAT ACTUALLY SAVES (9:15–22)

Now our author elaborates on why Christ's death was necessary:

> 15 Therefore he is the mediator of a new covenant, so that those who are called may receive the promised eternal inheritance, since a death has occurred that redeems them from the transgressions committed under the first covenant. 16 For where a will is involved, the death of the one who made it must be established. 17 For a will takes effect only at death, since it is not in force as long as the one who made it is alive. 18 Therefore not even the first covenant was inaugurated without blood. 19 For when every commandment of the law had been declared by Moses to all the people, he took the blood of calves and goats, with water and scarlet wool and hyssop, and sprinkled both the book itself and all the people, 20 saying, "This is the blood of the covenant that God commanded for you." 21 And in the same way he sprinkled with the blood both the tent and all the vessels used in worship. 22 Indeed, under the law almost everything is purified with blood, and without the shedding of blood there is no forgiveness of sins. (vv. 15–22)

6. What was made possible in these verses only by Christ's death, and how is that illustrated in verses 16–17?

7. We've seen the word *blood* numerous times in chapter 9. Just as the new covenant was established by blood, so was the old one, which we see in the author's reflections here from Exodus 24:3–8. What did the blood symbolize in both covenants?

8. According to Leviticus 17:11, why was blood effective in the ways God prescribed?

ONCE FOR ALL (9:23-28)

Pictured for us here is the all-important Day of Atonement. Once a year, the high priest took animal blood into the Most Holy Place, the inner chamber of the taberbacle, to atone for his own sins and then for the sins of God's people:

> 23 Thus it was necessary for the copies of the heavenly things to be purified
> with these rites, but the heavenly things themselves with better sacrifices than
> these. 24 For Christ has entered, not into holy places made with hands, which
> are copies of the true things, but into heaven itself, now to appear in the pres-
> ence of God on our behalf. 25 Nor was it to offer himself repeatedly, as the high
> priest enters the holy places every year with blood not his own, 26 for then he
> would have had to suffer repeatedly since the foundation of the world. But as
> it is, he has appeared once for all at the end of the ages to put away sin by the
> sacrifice of himself. 27 And just as it is appointed for man to die once, and after
> that comes judgment, 28 so Christ, having been offered once to bear the sins of
> many, will appear a second time, not to deal with sin but to save those who are
> eagerly waiting for him. (vv. 23–28)

9. Why do you think that the high priest had to repeat his sacrificial offering every year, whereas Jesus's sacrifice was needed only once, never to be repeated?

10. "Once" and "once for all" appear repeatedly in verses 23–28. The high priest went once a year into the Most Holy Place, and Jesus came to sacrifice himself for sin just once. What else in this passage is noted as being a single, one-time occurrence?

11. This is a good time to remember that our pastor-author is writing to struggling believers. How does he encourage them in verse 28 to persevere in their faith?

LET'S TALK

1. Some of the church's most beloved hymns sing of Jesus's shed blood, and we get a regular reminder of it when we participate in the Lord's Supper. Even so, it's not something we tend to talk about much. Discuss why blood is such a big deal in Hebrews 9 and why it's foundational to understanding the Christian faith.

2. We're told in verse 27 that "it is appointed for man to die once, and after that comes judgment." Talk about the full implication of these words, and then consider some ways to bring this reality into conversations with unbelieving friends or family members.

3. Under the old covenant, God accepted animal sacrifices as payment for sins, but this ritual couldn't purify a sinner's heart. Only one sacrifice, the blood of Jesus, could do that. His sacrifice washes "our conscience from dead works to serve the living God" (v. 14). Talk about why guilt blocks someone from serving God and why a conscience washed clean can freely serve. Describe your own experience.

WEEK 7

HOLDING FAST TO OUR HOPE

HEBREWS 10:1-39

We've been learning how Christ's sacrifice of himself fulfilled God's plan to redeem his people from sin. We see some of this again here, but it's not merely a repeat of what we've already learned. As one Bible teacher explains, "When an 'old' truth is being presented, some new light is always cast on it."[13] That's what's happening in Hebrews 10. The emphasis on Christ's sacrifice here is *our response*. How should God's people live in light of having such a great high priest, one who covered all our sins and failures? As we'll see, our life is to be marked by freedom, by faith, and by following in the way of our Savior.

A SHADOW OF GOOD THINGS (10:1-4)

We see a bit more now of why the old-covenant worship rituals were merely shadows of the blessings God intends for his people:

> 1 For since the law has but a shadow of the good things to come instead of the true form of these realities, it can never, by the same sacrifices that are continually offered every year, make perfect those who draw near. 2 Otherwise, would they not have ceased to be offered, since the worshipers, having once been cleansed, would no longer have any consciousness of sins? 3 But in these sacrifices there is a reminder of sins every year. 4 For it is impossible for the blood of bulls and goats to take away sins. (vv. 1–4)

1. How are worshipers described in verse 1?

2. The all-important Day of Atonement is clearly in mind again in verses 1–4. We remember that on this day, once a year, the high priest took sacrificial blood into the Most Holy Place, the inner chamber of the tabernacle, to atone for his sins and the sins of God's people. According to verses 3–4, what resulted from this annual occurrence?

GOD'S WILL (10:5–10)

Our pastor-author quotes the words of King David from Psalm 40:6–8 and presents them as the very words of Christ himself:

> 5 Consequently, when Christ came into the world, he said,
>
> "Sacrifices and offerings you have not desired,
> but a body have you prepared for me;
> 6 in burnt offerings and sin offerings
> you have taken no pleasure.
> 7 Then I said, 'Behold, I have come to do your will, O God,
> as it is written of me in the scroll of the book.'"
>
> 8 When he said above, "You have neither desired nor taken pleasure in sacrifices
> and offerings and burnt offerings and sin offerings" (these are offered according
> to the law), 9 then he added, "Behold, I have come to do your will." He does away
> with the first in order to establish the second. 10 And by that will we have been
> sanctified through the offering of the body of Jesus Christ once for all. (vv. 5–10)

3. Read David's words in Psalm 40:6–8. How does his wording help us understand what God wants most from his people—something that Jesus demonstrated so perfectly?

"The offering that God finds acceptable represents devotion from the heart. Sacrifices in themselves are powerless to please God or to secure a proper relationship between God and his people."[14]

OUT WITH THE OLD, IN WITH THE NEW (10:11-18)

Our author summarizes what he's been saying from the beginning of chapter 8 up until now. Christ's sacrifice has ushered in a whole new covenant—a relational bond—between God and his people:

> 11 And every priest stands daily at his service, offering repeatedly the same
> sacrifices, which can never take away sins. 12 But when Christ had offered
> for all time a single sacrifice for sins, he sat down at the right hand of God,
> 13 waiting from that time until his enemies should be made a footstool for
> his feet. 14 For by a single offering he has perfected for all time those who are
> being sanctified.
>
> 15 And the Holy Spirit also bears witness to us; for after saying,
>
> 16 "This is the covenant that I will make with them
> after those days, declares the Lord:
> I will put my laws on their hearts,
> and write them on their minds,"

17 then he adds,

> "I will remember their sins and their lawless deeds no more."

18 Where there is forgiveness of these, there is no longer any offering for sin. (vv. 11–18)

4. The old-covenant priests had to stand to offer sacrifices on a daily basis. How is that contrasted with Christ and his sacrifice in verses 11–12?

5. Notice the verb tenses in verse 14: "For by a single offering *he has* perfected for all time those who *are being* sanctified." What do these verb tenses show us about why we continue to struggle with sin even though our eternal destiny is sure?

6. Next, in verses 15–18, we find the long-ago promise of the new covenant from Jeremiah 31:33–34 (although it's clear here in Hebrews that the Holy Spirit is the one who inspired the prophet's words). What in verse 16 makes the new covenant so different from the old one?

7. According to verse 18, why does the new covenant that Christ ushered in make the old covenant obsolete?

Redemptive History in the Book of Hebrews[15]

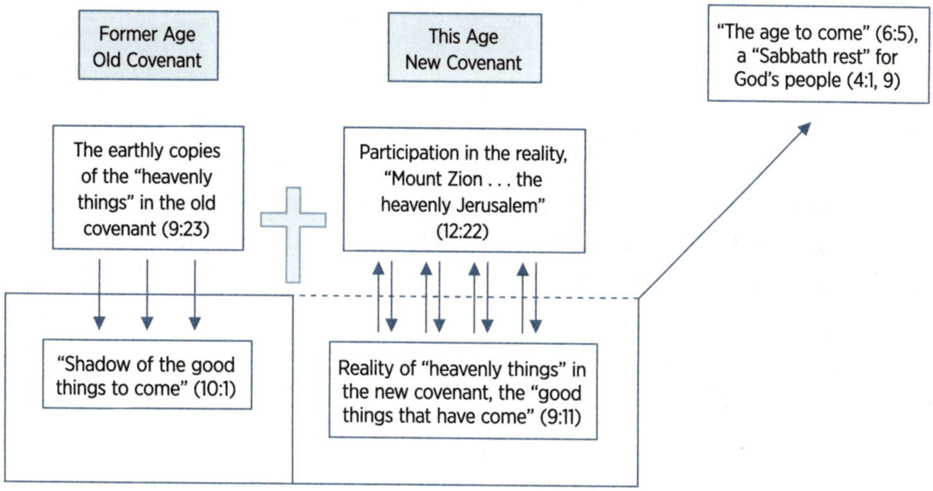

A NEW WAY OF LIFE (10:19–25)

Many preachers wrap up their sermons with an application, suggesting something for us to do in response to what we've heard. We have something like this beginning in verse 19:

> 19 Therefore, brothers, since we have confidence to enter the holy places by the
> blood of Jesus, 20 by the new and living way that he opened for us through
> the curtain, that is, through his flesh, 21 and since we have a great priest over
> the house of God, 22 let us draw near with a true heart in full assurance of
> faith, with our hearts sprinkled clean from an evil conscience and our bodies

washed with pure water. [23] Let us hold fast the confession of our hope without
wavering, for he who promised is faithful. [24] And let us consider how to stir
up one another to love and good works, [25] not neglecting to meet together, as
is the habit of some, but encouraging one another, and all the more as you see
the Day drawing near. (vv. 19–25)

8. Jesus our great high priest has abolished the need for continual sacrifices for sin and has ushered in a "new and living way" (v. 20). How did this change the way God's people can approach him?

9. Being sprinkled by the blood sacrifice of our great high priest, we can now draw near to God with a washed conscience. Why do you think a guilty conscience is a hindrance to drawing near to God?

10. The believers who first received this sermon-letter had been tempted to shrink back in fear, and the faith of some was faltering. Our author exhorts them to hold onto the hope that comes through Jesus. How do we put this into practice in verses 24–25?

GETTING SERIOUS ABOUT GOD'S WRATH (10:26–31)

Apparently, some of these wavering believers had stopped gathering with other Christians (v. 25), furthering their fall away from the faith altogether. Likely that is what underlies yet another sober warning:

> [26] For if we go on sinning deliberately after receiving the knowledge of the
> truth, there no longer remains a sacrifice for sins, [27] but a fearful expectation
> of judgment, and a fury of fire that will consume the adversaries. [28] Anyone
> who has set aside the law of Moses dies without mercy on the evidence of
> two or three witnesses. [29] How much worse punishment, do you think, will be
> deserved by the one who has trampled underfoot the Son of God, and has pro-
> faned the blood of the covenant by which he was sanctified, and has outraged
> the Spirit of grace? [30] For we know him who said, "Vengeance is mine; I will
> repay." And again, "The Lord will judge his people." [31] It is a fearful thing to fall
> into the hands of the living God. (vv. 26–31)

This is similar to the warning back in Hebrews 6. Both concern the sin of apostasy, which is a deliberate, willful, and persistent rejection of God and his ways. That's what our author means by "go on sinning deliberately" here in verse 26. And the particular sin he has in view is rejecting Jesus and his costly sacrifice.

11. What in verse 29 makes this particular sin so heinous?

12. It was bad enough when the old covenant was willfully violated, he says in verse 28. God sternly judged those violaters. What reason is given in verse 30 for why it is so much worse to reject the new covenant that Christ initiated by his death?

CONFIDENCE REWARDED (10:32–39)

As we've seen throughout, our author has a pastor's heart, so in typical fashion he follows his stern warning with encouragement:

> 32 But recall the former days when, after you were enlightened, you endured
> a hard struggle with sufferings, 33 sometimes being publicly exposed to reproach
> and affliction, and sometimes being partners with those so treated. 34 For you
> had compassion on those in prison, and you joyfully accepted the plundering
> of your property, since you knew that you yourselves had a better possession
> and an abiding one. 35 Therefore do not throw away your confidence, which has
> a great reward. 36 For you have need of endurance, so that when you have done
> the will of God you may receive what is promised. 37 For,
>
> "Yet a little while,
> and the coming one will come and will not delay;
> 38 but my righteous one shall live by faith,
> and if he shrinks back,
> my soul has no pleasure in him."
>
> 39 But we are not of those who shrink back and are destroyed, but of those who
> have faith and preserve their souls. (vv. 32–39)

13. The experience of persecution was nothing new for these wavering Christians. Why do you think this reminder of earlier days would be an effective means of encouraging them now?

14. What are these believers lacking, which has wreaked havoc on their confidence?

15. With a quote from Habakkuk 2:3–4, our author reminds his friends that living by faith is aligned with righteousness in God's eyes, but the opposite is also true: God is displeased with the one who "shrinks back" (v. 38). What does the author do in verse 39 to come alongside his friends and strengthen the encouragement he's been providing them?

LET'S TALK

1. Living a life of faith includes "not neglecting to meet together" (v. 25). Discuss what this means and how we are to apply this exhortation to our lives today.

2. There is a difference between sins we commit unintentionally and those we commit through a conscious, deliberate choice. Explain what Hebrews 10 teaches about the seriousness of deliberate sin. How are we both warned and encouraged about our sin in this chapter?

3. The Christian life is meant to be lived in and among other believers. It's God's plan—and his good gift—for maturing us spiritually. In this context, we are called to "stir up one another to love and good works" (v. 24). Discuss some practical ways you are doing this or ways you will begin to do it.

WEEK 8

PORTRAITS OF FAITH

HEBREWS 11:1-40

Over the years I've been blessed to know some godly women who greatly inspire me. As I observe their lives—the choices they make, the peace that characterizes their outlook, and their love for God's word—I want to be like them. What defines each one is a steady, abiding faith in Jesus. In his kindness, God places such people in our lives to help us grow spiritually and to show us what faith in action looks like. I hope you've experienced the blessing of godly role models! We find several in Hebrews 11. Pictured for us here are people from the Old Testament who exhibited great faith in God's promises. Our pastor-author points to these earlier believers to encourage his faltering friends to hold fast to Christ. If we had unlimited time, we could look back on all these fascinating stories in detail, but since we don't, I hope you'll choose at least one or two of them to read (see pp. 79–80 for the Hebrews 11 "Hall of Faith" chart). Let's approach this lesson with hearts seeking more of what the author aims to impart: vibrant, enduring faith.

FAITH DEFINED (11:1-2)

Having encouraged his friends to persevere in the faith, he now sets in their minds exactly what faith *is*:

> [1] Now faith is the assurance of things hoped for, the conviction of things not
> seen. [2] For by it the people of old received their commendation. (vv. 1–2)

1. What do you think is meant by "assurance" and "conviction" in this definition of faith?

2. The stage is set in verse 2 for everything that follows in chapter 11. What sort of "commendation" do you think our author is holding out here?

THE NECESSITY OF FAITH (11:3–7)

The nature of genuine faith is displayed for us in verses 3–7 from the time of creation until the days of Noah:

> [3] By faith we understand that the universe was created by the word of God, so that what is seen was not made out of things that are visible.
>
> [4] By faith Abel offered to God a more acceptable sacrifice than Cain, through which he was commended as righteous, God commending him by accepting his gifts. And through his faith, though he died, he still speaks. [5] By faith Enoch was taken up so that he should not see death, and he was not found, because God had taken him. Now before he was taken he was commended as having pleased God. [6] And without faith it is impossible to please him, for whoever would draw near to God must believe that he exists and that he rewards those who seek him. [7] By faith Noah, being warned by God concerning events as yet unseen, in reverent fear constructed an ark for the saving of his household. By this he condemned the world and became an heir of the righteousness that comes by faith. (vv. 3–7)

3. Skeptics argue that there's no way the universe and all of creation came about in a literal six-day period, as we're told in Genesis 1–2. Over the centuries, alternate theories have been suggested. Setting all this aside, what perspective on creation is rooted in faith according to verse 3?

The story of brothers Cain and Abel is found in Genesis 4. Cain was angry when the Lord rejected his offering and jealous because Abel's was approved, so Cain murdered Abel. Although details of the offerings are not provided in the biblical text, we can infer that the faith (or absence of faith) of each brother was a key factor in the acceptability of the sacrifices. Generations later came Enoch who, we're told in Genesis 5:22, 24, pleased God by walking closely with him.

4. Next comes Noah. How is his faith evidenced in verse 7?

5. We've been told that Jesus's sacrifice was designed by God to enable his people to draw near to him. How does verse 6 show us the part we play in enjoying this amazing privilege?

FAITH TAKES GOD AT HIS WORD (11:8–12)

The great patriarch Abraham is featured prominently among these heroes of faith:

> [8] By faith Abraham obeyed when he was called to go out to a place that he was to receive as an inheritance. And he went out, not knowing where he was going. [9] By faith he went to live in the land of promise, as in a foreign land, living in tents with Isaac and Jacob, heirs with him of the same promise. [10] For he was looking forward to the city that has foundations, whose designer and builder is God. [11] By faith Sarah herself received power to conceive, even when she was past the age, since she considered him faithful who had promised. [12] Therefore from one man, and him as good as dead, were born descendants as many as the stars of heaven and as many as the innumerable grains of sand by the seashore. (vv. 8–12)

6. Our author highlights portions of Abraham's life to show us particular ways that he demonstrated faith. What do you note about Abraham's faith in verses 8–12?

FAITH BELIEVES GOD'S PROMISES (11:13–16)

God made big promises to Abraham. The patriarch was to become a great nation through whom "all the families of the earth" would be blessed (Genesis 12:1–3). Later this promise was reaffirmed while Abraham was stargazing, and the Lord said to him, "Look toward heaven, and number the stars, if you are able to number them." Then he said to him, "So shall your offspring be." And Abraham "believed the LORD, and he counted it to him as righteousness" (Genesis 15:5–6). Abraham and his descendants are in view as our author continues:

> [13] These all died in faith, not having received the things promised, but having seen them and greeted them from afar, and having acknowledged that they were strangers and exiles on the earth. [14] For people who speak thus make it clear that they are seeking a homeland. [15] If they had been thinking of that

> land from which they had gone out, they would have had opportunity to return. [16] But as it is, they desire a better country, that is, a heavenly one. Therefore God is not ashamed to be called their God, for he has prepared for them a city. (vv. 13–16)

7. With faith in God's promises, Abraham structured his life as the Lord directed, even though he and his immediate descendants never reached the promised land. What kept their faith from wavering when these promises weren't realized?

FAITH RECEIVES BLESSING (11:17–22)

Our author gives us a few more key episodes in the lives of the patriarchs:

> [17] By faith Abraham, when he was tested, offered up Isaac, and he who had received the promises was in the act of offering up his only son, [18] of whom it was said, "Through Isaac shall your offspring be named." [19] He considered that God was able even to raise him from the dead, from which, figuratively speaking, he did receive him back. [20] By faith Isaac invoked future blessings on Jacob and Esau. [21] By faith Jacob, when dying, blessed each of the sons of Joseph, bowing in worship over the head of his staff. [22] By faith Joseph, at the end of his life, made mention of the exodus of the Israelites and gave directions concerning his bones. (vv. 17–22)

8. Even lacking the full details of these episodes, we can see that the faith of each patriarch was oriented toward the future. Why was that a mark of their faith?

FAITH CONQUERS FEAR (11:23–28)

Now our author moves forward in history to Moses, beginning with his birth and taking us to his leading Israel out of Egypt:

> 23 By faith Moses, when he was born, was hidden for three months by his parents,
> because they saw that the child was beautiful, and they were not afraid of the
> king's edict. 24 By faith Moses, when he was grown up, refused to be called the son
> of Pharaoh's daughter, 25 choosing rather to be mistreated with the people of God
> than to enjoy the fleeting pleasures of sin. 26 He considered the reproach of Christ
> greater wealth than the treasures of Egypt, for he was looking to the reward.
> 27 By faith he left Egypt, not being afraid of the anger of the king, for he endured
> as seeing him who is invisible. 28 By faith he kept the Passover and sprinkled the
> blood, so that the Destroyer of the firstborn might not touch them. (vv. 23–28)

9. Notice how many times our author prefaces his examples with the phrase "By faith…" How do you see faith demonstrated each time the phrase is used?

   - v. 23:

   - vv. 24–26:

   - v. 27:

   - v. 28:

Hebrews 11 "Hall of Faith"	
Abel	Genesis 4:1–16
Enoch	Genesis 5:18–24
Noah	Genesis 6–10
Abraham	Genesis 12:1–25:10
Sarah	Genesis 12:1–23:2
Isaac	Genesis 21–35
Jacob	Genesis 25–50
Joseph	Genesis 37–50
Moses	Exodus
Rahab	Joshua 2; 6:17–25
Barak	Judges 4–5
Gideon	Judges 6–8
Jephthah	Judges 11:1–12:7
Samson	Judges 13–16

Hebrews 11 "Hall of Faith"	
Samuel	1 Samuel 1:1–25:1
David	1–2 Samuel
The names below don't appear in Hebrews 11, but their history fits the descriptions in vv. 32–38.	
Elijah	1 Kings 17–19; 2 Kings 1–2
The widow of Zarephath	1 Kings 17:17–24
The Shunammite woman	2 Kings 4:18–37
Jeremiah	Jeremiah 20:2
Daniel	Daniel 3:19–28; 6:19–23
Zechariah	2 Chronicles 24:20–21
*extrabiblical tradition holds that Isaiah the prophet was sawn in two (v. 37)	

10. What connection can you make from these verses between faith and fear?

FAITH SEES DISPLAYS OF GOD'S POWER (11:29–31)

Our author takes us now to the miraculous crossing of the Red Sea and Israel's initial forays into the promised land of Canaan:

> [29] By faith the people crossed the Red Sea as on dry land, but the Egyptians,
> when they attempted to do the same, were drowned. [30] By faith the walls of
> Jericho fell down after they had been encircled for seven days. [31] By faith Rahab
> the prostitute did not perish with those who were disobedient, because she had
> given a friendly welcome to the spies. (vv. 29–31)

11. The people we see in verses 29–31 are noted for doing things that involved great risk. How does the author show in each case that the Lord viewed these actions as steps of faith?

FAITH FOCUSES FORWARD (11:32–40)

Our author could easily go on and on citing examples of great faith, but he wraps up with a brief recap from across the Old Testament, including some of the judges, King David, and the prophets:

> [32] And what more shall I say? For time would fail me to tell of Gideon, Barak,
> Samson, Jephthah, of David and Samuel and the prophets— [33] who through
> faith conquered kingdoms, enforced justice, obtained promises, stopped the
> mouths of lions, [34] quenched the power of fire, escaped the edge of the sword,
> were made strong out of weakness, became mighty in war, put foreign armies
> to flight. [35] Women received back their dead by resurrection. Some were tor-
> tured, refusing to accept release, so that they might rise again to a better life.
> [36] Others suffered mocking and flogging, and even chains and imprisonment.
> [37] They were stoned, they were sawn in two, they were killed with the sword.
> They went about in skins of sheep and goats, destitute, afflicted, mistreated—

[38] of whom the world was not worthy—wandering about in deserts and mountains, and in dens and caves of the earth.

[39] And all these, though commended through their faith, did not receive what was promised, [40] since God had provided something better for us, that apart from us they should not be made perfect. (vv. 32–40)

12. The Bible is unapologetically honest about the sins and shortcomings of Israel's leaders, including some who appear in verse 32. For that reason, we might wonder how these individuals make the cut and appear in this "heroes of faith" list. What does their inclusion here tell us?

13. Earlier in this list of the faithful, we were encouraged by how the Lord rewarded faith with miracles and powerful deliverances. That's not the case in verses 35–38. What lesson does this teach us about faith?

14. Surely those martyrs were blessed for their faith in ways we don't know, even though they "did not receive what was promised" (v. 39). The author is pointing out that they never saw the full unfolding of God's plan of redemption in the coming of Christ. What do we learn from verse 40 about God's intention in this regard?

LET'S TALK

1. Discuss the ways Hebrews 11 has enriched your understanding of faith and how God works through it.

2. At God's command, Abraham left his homeland, "and he went out, not knowing where he was going" (v. 8). Talk about what it means to take costly steps of obedience to God's word when you don't know how those steps will impact your life. Share a time when you've exercised your faith in costly obedience. How did it turn out for you?

3. We saw this week that faith triumphs over fear. Describe a time in your life when your faith conquered anxiety or fear.

WEEK 9

RUNNING OUR RACE

HEBREWS 12:1–29

If you've ever run a marathon, you know that significant training and personal discipline go into preparing for race day. If you want to make it to the finish line, you have to build up endurance, but you won't last through the sometimes painful exertion unless you keep your eye on the goal of crossing the finish line. We find this idea in Hebrews 12, where we see that God's fatherly care includes training us to endure the hardships of discipleship in order to enjoy the rewards awaiting us at the end of our earthly race. As we persevere, we find encouragement from Hebrews 12, which directs us to keep our eyes on our Savior, being mindful of all he endured to save us. Jesus anticipated the joy that awaited him, joy that far exceeded all his suffering along the way. The joy he anticipated is held out to us too, as we press on toward the prize of heaven.

LOOK TO JESUS (12:1–2)

Those "heroes" of faith from chapter 11, which we studied last week, were presented to the struggling Hebrews as role models of perseverance, just as they are for us today:

> 1 Therefore, since we are surrounded by so great a cloud of witnesses, let us
> also lay aside every weight, and sin which clings so closely, and let us run
> with endurance the race that is set before us, 2 looking to Jesus, the founder
> and perfecter of our faith, who for the joy that was set before him endured
> the cross, despising the shame, and is seated at the right hand of the throne
> of God. (vv. 1–2)

1. In addition to rejecting sin, our pastor-author calls believers to "lay aside every weight." What do you think he means by the "weight" we must set aside?

2. Endurance is possible when we fix our eyes on Jesus, focusing especially on how he lived his earthly life. In verse 2 we get a picture.

   - What did Jesus experience as he faced the cross?

   - What enabled him to endure it?

DISCIPLINED IN LOVE (12:3–11)

The first recipients of this letter had been getting a taste of the hostility that Jesus experienced, although, unlike Jesus, they hadn't been subjected to a horrific death. Even so, their faith was faltering. What they needed was the right spiritual perspective:

> 3 Consider him who endured from sinners such hostility against himself, so that
> you may not grow weary or fainthearted. 4 In your struggle against sin you have
> not yet resisted to the point of shedding your blood. 5 And have you forgotten
> the exhortation that addresses you as sons?
>
> "My son, do not regard lightly the discipline of the Lord,
> nor be weary when reproved by him.
> 6 For the Lord disciplines the one he loves,
> and chastises every son whom he receives."

7 It is for discipline that you have to endure. God is treating you as sons. For
what son is there whom his father does not discipline? 8 If you are left without
discipline, in which all have participated, then you are illegitimate children
and not sons. 9 Besides this, we have had earthly fathers who disciplined us and
we respected them. Shall we not much more be subject to the Father of spirits
and live? 10 For they disciplined us for a short time as it seemed best to them,
but he disciplines us for our good, that we may share his holiness. 11 For the
moment all discipline seems painful rather than pleasant, but later it yields the
peaceful fruit of righteousness to those who have been trained by it. (vv. 3–11)

3. Our author begins with a quote from Proverbs 3:11–12 to shape our perspective on suffering. How does he argue his case in verses 7–10?

4. What is God's purpose in all Christian suffering?

5. What attitude do you think is necessary to be "trained" by God's discipline?

DISCIPLINED FOR GOOD (12:12–17)

If we want to reap the results of God's fatherly discipline, we need more than the right attitude. We must also take action:

> 12 Therefore lift your drooping hands and strengthen your weak knees, 13 and
> make straight paths for your feet, so that what is lame may not be put out of
> joint but rather be healed. 14 Strive for peace with everyone, and for the holiness
> without which no one will see the Lord. 15 See to it that no one fails to obtain
> the grace of God; that no "root of bitterness" springs up and causes trouble,
> and by it many become defiled; 16 that no one is sexually immoral or unholy
> like Esau, who sold his birthright for a single meal. 17 For you know that after-
> ward, when he desired to inherit the blessing, he was rejected, for he found
> no chance to repent, though he sought it with tears. (vv. 12–17)

The idea of discipline presented in chapter 12 isn't punitive, like when parents discipline their kids for misbehaving. We want to remember that the viewpoint here is that of rigorous training, like when we prepare to run a marathon.

6. An important aspect of spiritual training is removing impediments from our lives. What do you think it means to "make straight paths for your feet, so that what is lame may not be put out of joint but rather be healed" (v. 13)?

7. Verses 14–16 involve training practices carried out in the fellowship of God's people. The pursuit of peace and holiness is key to building up both ourselves and our fellow believers. Bitterness, on the other hand, tears down. What is bitterness, and how do you think a "root of bitterness springs up"?

The good effects of spiritual discipline are blunted if we live to gratify our human appetites, whether for sex or some other fleshly pleasure. This is exactly what happened to Esau in Genesis. He was so focused on his craving for a good meal that he cast aside the promise of much greater blessing for immediate gratification. When the author writes that Esau sought repentance with tears, we aren't to think that he turned back to God and was rejected. God never turns away a truly repentant sinner! In Esau's case, he likely wanted to undo his rash action to regain the inheritance it had cost him.

> *"So long as Christians live as if the real is what can be touched, tasted, and grasped with the senses, as opposed to the realm of the spiritual which must be grasped by faith, they will not mature."*[16]

DISCIPLINED FOR ENDURANCE (12:18–24)

Another encouragement to endure in our Christian journey through life, hard as it may be, is what awaits us at the destination:

> 18 For you have not come to what may be touched, a blazing fire and dark-
> ness and gloom and a tempest 19 and the sound of a trumpet and a voice
> whose words made the hearers beg that no further messages be spoken to
> them. 20 For they could not endure the order that was given, "If even a beast
> touches the mountain, it shall be stoned." 21 Indeed, so terrifying was the
> sight that Moses said, "I tremble with fear." 22 But you have come to Mount
> Zion and to the city of the living God, the heavenly Jerusalem, and to in-
> numerable angels in festal gathering, 23 and to the assembly of the firstborn
> who are enrolled in heaven, and to God, the judge of all, and to the spirits
> of the righteous made perfect, 24 and to Jesus, the mediator of a new cove-
> nant, and to the sprinkled blood that speaks a better word than the blood
> of Abel. (vv. 18–24)

The manifestation of God's presence on Mount Sinai terrified Israel. When the Lord inaugurated the old covenant through Moses, the earth trembled and shook (take a look at Exodus 19:12–25).

8. As you read over Hebrews 12:18–24, how would you summarize the difference between God on Mount Sinai and God in the heavenly Jerusalem, and what makes the two experiences so different?

DON'T REFUSE HIM! (12:25–29)

We've been shown a God whose power, authority, and holiness are not to be trifled with or taken lightly:

> [25] See that you do not refuse him who is speaking. For if they did not escape
> when they refused him who warned them on earth, much less will we escape
> if we reject him who warns from heaven. [26] At that time his voice shook the
> earth, but now he has promised, "Yet once more I will shake not only the earth
> but also the heavens." [27] This phrase, "Yet once more," indicates the removal
> of things that are shaken—that is, things that have been made—in order that
> the things that cannot be shaken may remain. [28] Therefore let us be grateful
> for receiving a kingdom that cannot be shaken, and thus let us offer to God
> acceptable worship, with reverence and awe, [29] for our God is a consuming
> fire. (vv. 25–29)

9. Our author's friends must hold fast to their faith in the midst of suffering, and they must disregard temptations that can take hold during hard seasons. What specific temptation is warned against in verse 25, and who issues this warning?

10. God's presence shook Mount Sinai back in Moses's day, but at the end of the ages, the whole earth will shake. What is the purpose for this final shaking?

11. What exhortation does the author give to his frightened friends, and what hope is wrapped up in it?

LET'S TALK

1. Fixing our eyes on Jesus, we are called to "lay aside every weight, and sin which clings so closely" (v. 1). Can you identify a weight or weights in your own life that have hindered your race? How will you deal with them?

2. We're exhorted this week to "see to it... that no 'root of bitterness' springs up and causes trouble, and by it many become defiled" (v. 15). How can bitterness cause trouble, and how does one person's bitterness defile others? Talk about how you've experienced or witnessed the poison of bitterness.

3. The joys of heaven that await us are sure. As you run your faith race, do you live with the outlook prescribed in verse 28? There we are told, "Let us be grateful for receiving a kingdom that cannot be shaken." If we're honest, we have to admit that the struggles with the here and now of our daily lives sometimes sideline our gratitude for kingdom blessings. How would your responses to daily challenges be different if you viewed them through a kingdom-oriented lens? And how can you cultivate such a perspective in practical ways?

WEEK 10

NEVER FORSAKEN

HEBREWS 13:1–25

When circumstances are especially difficult, it's tempting to seek comfort in isolation, curled up under a blanket with a bowl of chips and a good movie. Appealing as that might be, we rob ourselves, and others too, if we regularly choose seclusion over fellowship with God's people. God designed us to thrive in the company of other Christians, so it's vital that we press in rather than withdraw during particularly hard seasons. That's what the author of Hebrews conveys as he wraps up his sermon-letter, what he calls his "word of exhortation" (13:22). Here we have concrete instructions for Christian living, ways we can encourage one another so that everyone thrives. With Jesus as our high priest, interceding for us and shepherding us toward our eternal home, we can live and love and serve God and people with hope-filled confidence, even in painful trials.

LOVE IN ACTION (13:1–6)

As our author prepares to wrap up the epistle, he lays out love in action. We mustn't allow difficult circumstances to hinder us from loving our brothers and sisters in Christ:

> 1 Let brotherly love continue. 2 Do not neglect to show hospitality to strangers,
> for thereby some have entertained angels unawares. 3 Remember those who
> are in prison, as though in prison with them, and those who are mistreated,
> since you also are in the body. 4 Let marriage be held in honor among all, and

let the marriage bed be undefiled, for God will judge the sexually immoral
and adulterous. [5] Keep your life free from love of money, and be content with
what you have, for he has said, "I will never leave you nor forsake you." [6] So
we can confidently say,

> "The Lord is my helper;
> I will not fear;
> what can man do to me?" (vv. 1–6)

1. First on this list of practical ways to love is hospitality. In ancient Near Eastern culture, showing hospitality was a big deal. Guests were offered the very best, no matter the cost to the host. Our author thinks back to when Abraham welcomed strangers with a lavish meal and every comfort he could provide (Genesis 18:1–8). Unbeknownst to Abraham, his guests were angels in human form, sent by God! Why do you think that hospitality is a powerful demonstration of love?

2. What attitude or feeling is our pastor-author highlighting in verse 3?

"God identifies himself with his people and will never abandon them to their own limited resources."[17]

3. Next on the list is sexual purity, specifically as it concerns marriage. How are believers to view marriage—not just their own but the marriage of others as well?

4. It's clear from verse 5 that love of money breeds discontentment. Why do you think love of money and discontentment go hand in hand?

5. From the Old Testament quotes in verses 5–6, what is the foundation of lasting contentment?

SEEKING THE CITY TO COME (13:7–17)

More instructions follow, with Jesus once again serving as our example:

> 7 Remember your leaders, those who spoke to you the word of God. Consider
> the outcome of their way of life, and imitate their faith. 8 Jesus Christ is the
> same yesterday and today and forever. 9 Do not be led away by diverse and
> strange teachings, for it is good for the heart to be strengthened by grace, not
> by foods, which have not benefited those devoted to them. 10 We have an altar
> from which those who serve the tent have no right to eat. 11 For the bodies of

those animals whose blood is brought into the holy places by the high priest as
a sacrifice for sin are burned outside the camp. 12 So Jesus also suffered outside
the gate in order to sanctify the people through his own blood. 13 Therefore let
us go to him outside the camp and bear the reproach he endured. 14 For here
we have no lasting city, but we seek the city that is to come. 15 Through him
then let us continually offer up a sacrifice of praise to God, that is, the fruit of
lips that acknowledge his name. 16 Do not neglect to do good and to share what
you have, for such sacrifices are pleasing to God.

17 Obey your leaders and submit to them, for they are keeping watch over
your souls, as those who will have to give an account. Let them do this with
joy and not with groaning, for that would be of no advantage to you. (vv. 7–17)

6. The blessing of biblically sound leaders is especially vital during times of difficulty, when faith is tested. What three approaches toward faithful leaders are advocated in verse 7?

Because "Jesus Christ is the same yesterday and today and forever" (v. 8), he will never abandon his people. For that reason, Christians must not fall back into old-covenant rituals or follow "strange" new teachings that contradict Christ's all-sufficient sacrifice. The "strange teachings" in verse 9 seem to have involved food rituals of some kind, likely tied to old-covenant sacrifices. Some of those sacrifices included feasting on portions of the slain animal as a sign of peace with God. On the Day of Atonement, however, the animal carcasses weren't eaten. Instead, they were taken outside the camp and burned. This particular ritual pointed forward to Jesus, who was taken "outside the gate" of Jerusalem to be crucified (v. 12).

7. Look again at verses 13–15. What attitude and outlook is to characterize our Christian life?

8. How are believers to live under the authority of their spiritual leaders, and why?

WELL EQUIPPED (13:18–25)

The author of this epistle is unknown to us, but he clearly knows those to whom he is writing. He gets personal as he draws the letter to a close with a prayer request and a beautiful benediction, a blessing, on his friends:

> 18 Pray for us, for we are sure that we have a clear conscience, desiring to act
> honorably in all things. 19 I urge you the more earnestly to do this in order that
> I may be restored to you the sooner. 20 Now may the God of peace who brought
> again from the dead our Lord Jesus, the great shepherd of the sheep, by the
> blood of the eternal covenant, 21 equip you with everything good that you may
> do his will, working in us that which is pleasing in his sight, through Jesus
> Christ, to whom be glory forever and ever. Amen.
>
> 22 I appeal to you, brothers, bear with my word of exhortation, for I have
> written to you briefly. 23 You should know that our brother Timothy has been
> released, with whom I shall see you if he comes soon. 24 Greet all your leaders
> and all the saints. Those who come from Italy send you greetings. Grace be
> with all of you. (vv. 18–25)

9. From the benediction in verses 20–21, list everything noted about God and what he did and does.

10. The epistle has taught us a lot about the old covenant, especially the practice of the priesthood and how the priests carried out their ministry. According to verse 20, how is the new covenant—the one we live under with Christ as our great high priest—different from the old one?

LET'S TALK

1. In full-on pastor mode, our author leaves his readers with action steps, points of application to step out and do. His instructions include things like hospitality, money, contentment, and marriage. Which of these exhortations do you find most convicting or challenging—and why?

2. In verse 4 we're instructed, "Let marriage be held in honor among all." Talk about what it means to honor a marriage—whether your own or someone else's—and the institution of marriage in general.

3. As we come to the end of Hebrews, note what you've learned or what's affected you most about:

   - The character of God

   - The gospel of salvation through Jesus Christ

   - The path of discipleship

HELPFUL RESOURCES FOR STUDYING HEBREWS

Hughes, Philip Edgcumbe. *A Commentary on the Epistle to the Hebrews*. Eerdmans, 1977.

Johnson, Dennis E. *Hebrews*. In *Hebrews–Revelation*, 19–217. Vol. 12 of *ESV Expository Commentary*. Edited by Iain M. Duguid, James M. Hamilton Jr., and Jay Sklar. Crossway, 2018.

Johnson, Dennis E. *Perfect Priest for Weary Pilgrims: A Theology of Hebrews*. New Testament Theology. Crossway, 2024.

Jones, Hywel R. *Let's Study Hebrews*. Banner of Truth, 2002.

Lane, William L. *Hebrews: A Call to Commitment*. Regent College, 1985.

Lloyd-Jones, Martyn. *A Merciful and Faithful High Priest: Studies in the Book of Hebrews*. Crossway, 2017.

Schrock, David S. *The Royal Priesthood and the Glory of God*. Short Studies in Biblical Theology. Crossway, 2022.

Stevens, Daniel. *Songs of the Son: Reading the Psalms with the Author of Hebrews*. Crossway, 2025.

NOTES

1. William L. Lane, *Hebrews: A Call to Commitment* (Regent College, 1985), 26.
2. Summarized from Phil Johnson, "Angels: Messengers and Ministers of God," Ligonier, July 1, 2007, https://www.ligonier.org/.
3. Lane, *Hebrews*, 41.
4. Lane, *Hebrews*, 42 (emphasis in original).
5. Hywel R. Jones, *Let's Study Hebrews* (Banner of Truth, 2002), 25.
6. Burk Parsons, "What Is Propitiation?," podcast transcript, Ligonier, May 27, 2021, https://learn.ligonier.org/.
7. Lane, *Hebrews*, 75 (emphasis in original).
8. Dennis E. Johnson, *Hebrews*, in *Hebrews–Revelation*, vol. 12 of *ESV Expository Commentary*, ed. Iain M. Duguid, James M. Hamilton Jr., and Jay Sklar (Crossway, 2018), 82.
9. Jones, *Let's Study Hebrews*, 68.
10. John Piper, "Jesus: From Melchizedek to Eternal Savior," sermon, Desiring God, December 1, 1996, https://www.desiringgod.org/.
11. Piper, "Jesus: From Melchizedek to Eternal Savior."
12. "The Tabernacle Tent" diagram adapted from p. 186 of the *ESV® Study Bible* (The Holy Bible, English Standard Version®), © 2008 by Crossway, a publishing ministry of Good News Publishers. Used by permission. All rights reserved.
13. Jones, *Let's Study Hebrews*, 107.
14. Lane, *Hebrews*, 134.
15. "Redemptive History in the Book of Hebrews" diagram from p. 2375 of the *ESV® Study Bible* (The Holy Bible, English Standard Version®), © 2008 by Crossway, a publishing ministry of Good News Publishers. Used by permission. All rights reserved.
16. Lane, *Hebrews*, 169.
17. Lane, *Hebrews*, 175.

Flourish Bible Study Series

Old Testament

Judges

Esther

Job

The Psalms of Ascents

Ecclesiastes

Jonah

Habakkuk

New Testament

Luke

Romans

Ephesians

Philippians

Colossians

Hebrews

James

1–2 Peter

For more information, visit **crossway.org**.